Ajax's Whimsical Revolution

By Paul Brodie

Cover image by Paul Brodie and Markus Hannonen

ISBN-13:978-1482769050

Table of Contents

Introduction

A few months ago I switched blog platforms. With the platform switch I also changed my blog style, slightly. Leaving my old persona of Ajax behind wasn't easy, though, so I compiled my favorite posts from the blog I had kept for two years, Ajax's Whimsical Revolution, and submitted it for ePublication on Amazon's Kindle Platform. The 78 posts selected have been available in that format for a while and I've decided it is time to add a trade paperback print option version through Amazon affiliate CreateSpace.

The purpose of this book is to fulfill a lifelong dream of publishing a book. With the current state of our national economy and the employment crisis, my two college degrees aren't helping me much, so I've begun to seriously pursue my dream career of writing. Since publishing this book in its "e" form I have self-published an allegorical novelette and have several other book projects underway. I still blog regularly at PaulBrodie.WordPress.com, and have even started developing a collection of comic drawings, trying my hand at being a cartoonist.

Within these pages you'll find some well written essays, some jumbled thoughts, some humorous observations and hopefully a fun read. I don't have answers to major life questions or problems, maybe I do, but I think those are things best discovered on an individual basis. All I can do is contribute my opinion, in my voice, and this book is one way that I have tried to do that. I hope you enjoy the read.

-Paul Brodie, March 2012

Waking up is the worst part of the day

I really don't like waking up. Especially when the temperature outside is 70 degrees less than the temperature inside. My alarm sings the "Psych" theme song and I wake up, but then I remember that old Christmas classic, "the weather outside is frightful, and my bed is so delightful..." or something like that. Anyway, I'll give you two good reasons why waking up is the worst part of the day.

1. Elementary school playground logic - Sleeping is comfortable and stress free, being awake is less of each of those. This discrepancy causes cognitive dissonance. We are happy while asleep, but we are waking up, and probably would prefer to stay asleep, which means our actions are not in line with our thinking, hence the dissonance. How do we deal with dissonance? Rationalization! We rationalize by adding a new cognition, or thought. This is why I like to use elementary school playground logic. Remember this "first is the worst, second is the best, third is the one with the hairy chest"? This is adding a new cognition. In order to feel good about yourself when you come in second in the race for the swings at recess, you sing this little song to the person who beat you, and for good measure you alienate the person who came in right after you (makes perfect sense). Anyway, I add this cognition, and it works, because the first thing I do each day is wake up, practically speaking. Technically you could say the first thing I do is sleep, as I am asleep at midnight when the calendar says it is a new day. But to embrace that idea would be to harsh on my buzz from harshing on waking up. If I acknowledge that the first thing I do each day is sleep for 6 hours, how do I have any ground to stand my complaints on? To sum it up, the first thing I do is wake up, and first is the worst.

2. The thermal retention dynamic - It is winter and there aren't any degrees of temperature outside. Zero. Ice and snow cover the ground and not long after I've walked out my door ice covers the inside of my nose and lungs as well. When an object enters an environment, if the environment is warmer, the object becomes warmer; if the environment is colder then the object becomes colder. I am the object in this case, and I don't like to become colder. How does this relate to waking up? Well, shortly after waking up I need to go outside to go to the gym and then to classes. By staying in bed I am able to experience the thermal retention dynamic, which is, I don't get cold.

At this point, you must be thinking that I'm quite the complaining baby-pants. You are correct to assume that. I am not ashamed. There are certain things that aren't worth actually worrying about; this waking up thing is one of them. I will do it regardless of whether I want to or not, because, truth is, I love being awake, for a time. Waking up is the worst part of the day, that means it gets better throughout the day, i.e., no part of the day is worse than waking up. Really this wasn't complaining at all (adding a cognition), this has been a celebration of the rest of the day. As I said, some things just aren't worth worrying about, so instead of carrying those thoughts all day and stressing out, it is helpful for me to process them and rid them from my working memory. Type it up and click "publish post" and now it is your problem, not mine. Good day, neighbor!

Nutrition for all!

I love to eat, but I hate to grocery shop and prepare food. I love restaurants. If I had sufficient funds, I would never buy real groceries. I'd buy all those freezer/microwave deals and lots of cookies, maybe some real fruit, but not meal ingredients. Give me *I.H.O.P.* for breakfast, *Subway* for lunch and *Chili's* for dinner - sometimes *Texas Roadhouse*. I think I could make those rounds every day and be happy. As it stands, I'm throwing things together out of convenience and based on taste. This afternoon, for example, I arrived home and didn't feel like preparing food, so I dropped a pair of brown sugar *Pop-Tarts* into the toaster and washed a golden delicious apple - dinner! Yesterday I ate a salad (lettuce, carrots, green peppers, tomato, cucumber, *Cool Ranch Doritos* [crushed], cubed ham, shredded cheese and ranch dressing). That was all for the entire day, unless you count *Cadbury Cream Eggs*, I had a few of those. Friday I ate one of my specialties: rice with cream of chicken soup, canned chicken, black olives, peas, pineapple and hot sauce. This is my standby. I'll make up a bunch of that and eat it for a week. But that's all I ate that day, along with an apple fritter I picked up on campus on my way to class, but that was all. Somehow I remain alive and feel pretty good most of the time. It really is amazing what our bodies can survive on.

I'm not saying that eating the way I do doesn't, or won't ever, have an effect on me. At least, according to the TV and nutrition gods, I assume eating the way I do will result in poor health, sooner or later. But maybe not, maybe we are getting jerked around, maybe candy and cookies and pizza aren't so bad after all. I feel pretty good, I sleep well, and I go to the gym every morning...*and* exercise. Maybe I don't need to meet the requirements of the food pyramid. I guess I'll know if tomorrow morning there is a brick with a food pyramid cut off the back of a cereal box rubber-banded to it thrown through my front window. I don't think that will be enough to get my attention though, no, it will take more than that. They will have to send goons to my front door with a coupon for oatmeal, or something. I will continue to eat horrendously. As long as I look and feel healthy, I will keep on my path of convenience food, with the occasional burst of apples and salad. *Pop-Tarts*, *Cadbury* Easter candy and *Dove* dark chocolate have gotten me this far in life, I can't give up on them now.

I think I eat pretty well actually; I just don't like the purchasing and preparing aspects. I do like candy and donuts, I can't (or won't) help that. I don't know what good any of this does for anyone, especially me, but especially you. I will now fry up a can of chicken with some barbeque sauce and cheese. Eat that dieticians and food guide folks! I know I will.

Quote of the day

Change your thoughts and you change your world. - Norman Vincent Peale

I just need to post something since I haven't for a few days. Today is April 1, though this post will show up as a few days ago because I created it then, just by pasting the quote from that day in this thing. I thought about responding to the quote with some of my "philosophizing" but I don't really feel like it anymore. The quote is very George Kelly, however, who I am reading about today in preparation for the personality psychology test I need to take tomorrow. Kelly was the topic of class a few weeks ago, but why read it then when the test is still 2 weeks out?

So here I am, reading three weeks of class material in 2 days in order to score a mid 70's grade on the test. This is how I do it. I've gotten a 90 and two 70's range grades on exams for that class so far. I don't think I ever worried much about grades; they have always come easily enough for me. Even in this class, my exam average isn't A material, but with the papers we've written I have an 87% for the class. With this final exam and the final paper it is possible that I could pull off an A- for the semester. Which is why I am putting some effort into preparing for this test. I don't care if I end up with an A or B in the class, so long as I pass it, which I will. When the possibility of an A is high, and the goal proximity is close, I am OK with changing my thoughts to change my world, and put some more effort into it.

We discussed Taoism in this class the last two times we met. I think I am pretty Taoist in the way I operate. I go with the natural flow, not in laziness, but in what feels right. If I am tired I sleep, hungry I eat, done with studying I stop. That sentence isn't structured properly I suppose. Change your thought change my sentence structure. I like the Taoist approach of not forcing things. If it needs to get done you just submit to the Way and do what you need to when you feel you need to. It is less stressful, that's for sure. It is finals time for the semester and so many students are getting burnt out and stressed out. I am annoyed and frustrated as well, but not with classes, what a useless thing, in my opinion, to be stressed out about. I have to go now.

Two blocks and a slight breeze

A few days ago I visited Taco Bell. While visiting I decided to have something to eat. I ordered two Crunchwraps, two Cheesy Potato burritos and one caramel apple empanada. I took the food home with me to eat. I didn't check the bag to see if everything was in there, so of course it wasn't all in there. When I got home I realized that they had forgotten the empanada; I checked the receipt, they hadn't forgotten to charge me for it. Oh well, this stuff happens. I mentioned it to Muffin Man and he said "Go back and demand justice!" To which I responded, "Two blocks [how far Taco Bell is from my apartment], 50 MPH wind, 20 degree wind-chill; the revolution doesn't cover that!"My sage friend waxed philosophical at that point, "It's funny how easily revolutions can be thwarted by two blocks and a slight breeze."

I don't know if that was worth mentioning, but two blocks and a slight breeze seemed like it would make a good title. Plus I'm typing up an assignment and you know how well I focus. I don't. That's how.

Ajax vs. Vending Machine

A month or so ago I was just finishing up the stock pile of *Butterfinger* bars my brother and sister-in-law sent in a package for Christmas. My brother works for *Nestle/Purina*, so he gets the goods at employee rates. Sweet deal (get it? sweet, candy, that's right). I ate the last *Butterfinger* and thought it was the greatest thing ever, I don't know why. The next day after classes I went to the vending machine to get a *Butterfinger*. Before I continue, I'd just like to mention that last semester the candy bars in the machine were 85 cents, this semester they are 100 cents. Ridiculous. I still buy them though. This is exactly why they are 100 cents now. I digress.

The vending machines have a card reader for our school ID card. I swipe the card and make my selection and bammo! Two candy bars drop. At first my thoughts said "woo hoo!" a la Homer Simpson, and then my thoughts said "D'oh!" a la Homer Simpson. A wave of "that second candy bar isn't yours, you didn't pay for it" came over me. I picked up both bars and put them in my coat pocket and began my 3/4 mile walk home.

The entire walk I debated on what I should do with that second candy bar. At first I thought I could walk into the administration building and ask to see the president of the college (at other schools he'd be a dean, I guess, but we call him president). I decided that was too much. Then I thought I could go to the food services people and give them the candy bar, but I didn't know where to go to do that. I figured there was probably a phone number for the vending service somewhere on the machine, but that seemed like a lot of work. Just before I got home I realized that the second bar slipping down left an empty space in the spiral candy holding pushing deal. I could just go back, swipe my card, make the selection, the corkscrew would roll and nothing would drop. The machine would take my money and we'd be square. I was content with that plan and continued home happy. When I got home I didn't feel like eating the candy bar(s) so I stashed 'em in the desk.

I discussed the dilemma with one of my roommates, who said he didn't think it was a big deal. I also discussed it with another friend and she found my concern over it amusing, as did I. Eventually, the next day came, on the next day. I was slightly afraid that the vending machine would already have taken some unsuspecting sucker's money, but happily, after making the trip to the building especially for the purpose of squaring my business with the machine, I found that the empty slot was still present. I smiled and swiped my card. Made the selection. The corkscrew spun and stopped. It was finished. Then the corkscrew spun again and another candy bar dropped. Defeated, I eventually added the third Butterfinger bar to my new collection. I was beaten; the machine was too smart for me.

I continued to spend way more time than necessary (or healthy) thinking about the dilemma. To recap, I have spent $2 and received 3 candy bars...when I spell it out, I'm really the one getting ripped off, but that's another story. I don't remember now when the new idea came to me, possibly in the shower (where I do a lot of thinking) or during a daydream in class, or possibly in an epiphanal moment where I sprang up in my bed at 3am with the cure for cancer and then this candy bar dilemma pushed that out and I said "Eureka!" No matter how the idea came, it came.

The day after the last vending machine transaction I put this new plan into play. I faced the machine, card in hand. I eyed the empty slots in the machine. I had to choose the right one. If I chose a slot that was always empty, it might not work, the machine might not be programmed to use those slots. Luckily, it was nearing the end of the week and the *Peanut M&M's* were all out. I slid the card, made the selection for the empty row and the corkscrew spun, but to no avail for me. The digital display read "vend out: make selection." I couldn't believe it. Even in my attempt to pay for an invisible candy bar to the end of squaring my deal with the machine, I was thwarted. Depressed from this defeat, I bought a Butterfinger bar to comfort me.

[Author's note: A few weeks after the final episode of the *Butterfinger Boppo* (as it will be called in the history books), I attempted to purchase a drink from the machine next to the one discussed above. I pushed the buttons and it made a noise, but the little doors never sprung open to drop my drink. It didn't say make selection, it did take my money. Though the drink machine now owes me 50 cents, I'm willing to call it even and forget the whole mess.]

She Loves Me and I Didn't Even Know It...or Her

Last night when I checked my e-mail I had this message:

Hello My Dear,

My name is Rebecca I am very intrested to your profilein(www.purevolume.com)i will like to know you, I will like you to send me an email to my private address (rebeccanelson200@yahoo.com) so that i can give you my pictures for you to know whom i am. I believe after then we will know each other very well, Remember colour or distance means nothing rather true LOVE,HONEST,CARING and UNDERSTANDING matters allot in every human life.I will be waiting to read from you soon,Take good care of your self and all that belong to you over there bye.Here is my email address again (rebeccanelson200@yahoo.com)

Your in love

Rebecca

Obviously I replied right away, sending my phone number, address, mother's maiden name and bank account information. When it comes to true love, you can't hold anything back. After all, what really matters is "true LOVE, HONEST, CARING and UNDERSTANDING." I couldn't have said it better myself...psych! A 4 year old could have said it better. Here is my response to Rebecca, my "in love":

Dear Rebecca,

Thank you for your interest in my purevolume.com page. I understand that simply seeing a picture of me and hearing me play a few songs is enough to capture the heart of even the coldest person alive, but what you are feeling isn't love. You are the victim of my uncontrollable and impossible-to-tame charm. It happens to the best of them. Why, just last week I received three e-mails similar to yours from world leaders; it was the same situation, they saw me on purevolume and bam! Actually, the Royal Danish Consulate General saw me on Facebook, not purevolume, but to the same end.

I'm sure you are a great girl, not one of those crazy computer-script generated chain-mail sneak in a virus or steal your identity types. I can tell by your horrific use of the English language. I hope with all of my heart that English is not your first language, or even second, for if it is, there is no hope for the future of this world.

Once again, I am flattered that you would pick me out from the countless number of potential targets for your fraud. I wish you the best...in prison. I hear they've got Skittles in the vending machine there now.

Your pal,

Ajax

Sticking it to Tooth Decay, Cool Mint Style

[While searching for the sonnet attempt I mentioned in the previous post, I found this instead, an old free write I did for an English class. I think it is humorous, but I laugh at my own stuff pretty easily. I will have to type in that sonnet sometime, maybe this afternoon. -Ajax]

In a world of extreme sports and maximum strength pain relievers, where everything is a competition and buzz-words and action-adjectives make everything more appealing, enter the *Extreme* toothbrush and toothpaste. Brushing your teeth is no longer a bedtime routine, it is an adventure. Commercials for oral care products feature beautiful people and adrenaline pumping (OK, maybe not) computer animation of plaque and "teeth staining" being blasted away by cool-mint laser beams of mouthwash. Tooth decay just doesn't stand a chance anymore. Not in my mouth anyway, especially not since I saw the commercials for the new Oral-B® CrossAction® Pro-Health™ tooth brush and Crest's Pro-Health toothpaste. "Why just brush your teeth when you can clean your whole mouth?" Why, indeed.

I was convinced by the end of the commercial, 100% sold, I needed that toothbrush. My current one, store brand, was showing its wear; the bristles are flayed out in every direction and are fading fast, indicating it is time for a new brush. Two nights ago I purchased the brush, the manual version, for $3.19. In my opinion, it is living up to its hype. The package boasts of 7 oral care benefits: removes hard to reach plaque, reduces gingivitis, cleans along the gum line, polishes away surface stains, removes odor-causing germs on the tongue, stimulates gums and is gentle on enamel and gums. According to the website (footnote 1), in clinical studies the CrossAction® brush removes up to 90% more plaque and provides 55% better gum care than the competition manual toothbrush. Throw in the CrissCross® Power Tip® Bristles and soft gum stimulators and you have yourself a prepared-for-anything dental hygiene tool. I am going to destroy plaque and "odor-causing" tongue germs.

A good brush is only part of the battle; CrossAction® gets you into the battle zone, Crest Pro-Health provides the ammunition. "Using breakthrough technology, Crest Pro-Health Toothpaste is the first and only toothpaste on the market today to contain the Polyfluorite System™," boasts the Crest website. It has a Polyfluorite System™? Oh, yeah – though I don't know what that means. It sounds like it will clean my teeth. The box features a high-tech looking diagram of teeth, covered with a grid system to pinpoint the location of the paste's benefits: fights cavities, fights plaque, fights gingivitis, builds increasing protection against painful sensitivity (only the tooth kind of sensitivity, sadly), fights tartar, whitens teeth by removing surface stains and freshens breath. All I have to say to that is this, "wow, they thought of everything." All it cost me was $2.79.

At the end of the day, I feel comfortable knowing that my mouth is safe. The glossy metallic-blue packaging used to protect my weapons until the time they were unleashed now lies at the bottom of a trash bucket. The commercials are over and the buzz-words forgotten, but man, my mouth is clean.

Tales from a Psychology Class

Today our professor shared a story with us about one of his daughters from when she was three. He was in the middle of a four month stint in China, working on research. One day his wife called to say that their daughter was hallucinating. She told him the daughter was saying that she heard voices in her head. She was being told what to do and what to think about. My professor said he was slightly worried as she was pretty young and shouldn't be having those kinds of problems. It never became an issue and all went along with the "voices" not being talked about as much anymore.

After the time in China was complete, my professor returned home. He decided to talk to his daughter about the voices. He asked if she heard a voice like mommy's or daddy's; she said it was like mommy's. Then he asked if it was like mommy or like a little girl; she said it was like a little girl. He asked if she heard a lot of voices or just one; she only heard one voice. He then asked if the voice was like her's or someone else's; it was like her voice. The daughter then said, "it is my voice!"

This was how she developed an understanding of thinking. I thought this was a neat developmental account of learning to think. Does language start inside of our minds, or outside of us through our interaction with others? Babies learn the language of their parents, which lends to the source of language being socially learned. I don't think we can definitively say that language is innately or socially learned, as an all inclusive determination. There are biological functions that need to be working for language to develop, but a lot of it is social as well. Because so much of our learning is from an outside-in approach, it makes sense that a child might have an experience like this when they begin to think silently. When children learn to read, they sound things out. The process of hearing themselves say the sounds helps them organize those sounds as words, which are labels for things in the environment. I think it is all quite interesting. That's all. What? I don't have anything profound to say. I was just relating some thoughts. Go watch TV.

Ideas like This are What Makes it Hard for Me to Pay Attention in Class

We were talking about the history of policing in Criminal Justice recently. The instructor mentioned 1360 BC Egypt. He said 99% of the people of Egypt lived along the Nile River; naturally, that's where the criminals would be as well. He said the Pharaoh's army would police the river. I wrote in my notes "Nile River Highway Patrol." The river was their highway. That reminded me of the television show CHiP's. The late '70's or early '80's police drama/sit-com. I don't know if it was a drama or a comedy, all I know is every episode ended with a freeze frame laugh. I liked the show because I was young and liked police things. Anyway, if you are familiar with the show you know it has a degree of cheesiness to it. Here's my idea for a TV show: Nile River Highway Patrol. You get two disco studs and dress them in the ancient Egyptian equivalent of TV motorcycle patrolman uniforms and put them in a boat. Although the year and environment would be much different, the storylines would be basically the same, just adapt the crimes to meet the circumstances. The dialogue would all be '70's era, it'd be fantastic! Maybe I'm wrong, but I think I'd like to see this show.

Of course, this idea will only fly if Erik Estrada is willing to play the Pharaoh.

The Caped Crusader vs. the Caped Instigator

Bruce Wayne and the Phantom of the Opera: A Case Study

Batman and the Phantom are both victims of childhood trauma. Each wears a mask and acts in supernatural ways, but they are even more different than they are alike. Batman is a less musical, more selfless version of the Phantom. It might not be fair at all to compare these two, as their lots in life are very different, but they are just make believe, so it doesn't matter.

Batman (as depicted in Christopher Nolan's movie *Batman Begins*, I'm not a comic book purist, sorry if you are) falls in a hole and has bats fly by him. On top of that he witnesses his parents being shot in a robbery. These events are enough to strain anyone and greatly influence the course of their life. Batman chose not to let the trials conquer him; he saw the problems of society which caused his misfortune and decided to fight them. In a selfless manner he risks his life for the good of the whole. If I inherited billions of dollars, I'd probably be more willing to give as well. On the matter of selflessness, does Batman ever really give up his grudge? Maybe he isn't so selfless after all...

The Phantom of the Opera, now he was a tormented person. While Batman's experiences were terribly traumatic, they were isolated incidents, which isn't to say the effect wasn't long lasting, but the experience itself wasn't. The Phantom, however, was treated as an animal for years: caged, beaten and ridiculed. Can it be any surprise that he spends his life in solitude, composing amazing music? No. When he hangs a man, crashes a chandelier (again, based on the movie and listening to the score) and abducts a young woman, is there any surprise?

Batman's experience left him inside of society; he saw both sides of it, good and bad. The Phantom was taken away from the good side of society and saw only the very worst. It could be said that Batman rose above his circumstances to be the anti-hero, while the Phantom succumbed to the "music of the night" to become an infestation.

They both break the law; they both seek to fulfill their own wants above others, at least for the first part of the movie. In a selfish way each masked figure carries out his form of justice, but in the end, Batman burns down his house and the Phantom lets Kristine and the blonde guy leave in the swan head canoe. I really didn't think this through anymore than that Batman was a more selfless, less musical version of the Phantom, which now, after typing this much, I think have unconvinced myself of Batman's altruism. He's the same as the rest of us, they both are. Except for the masks, living in caves and never needing to eat, sleep or breathe clean air.

A Long Paragraph Regarding My Thoughts on Welfare

Receiving something you did not earn is not good for you. Let me rephrase, receiving the basic necessities of life without earning them is never good for you. Receiving gifts is good, the ones from your family and friends, as they are (hopefully) a token of appreciation, friendship or love. These are good feelings to express and I am not against giving gifts in order to express them. I am against giving someone a "free ride." People might think I'm just jealous, or look at the benefits I've received and think I'm being whiny or acting like an elitist. If I am, perhaps it is because of those benefits I have received? Look at children, we can learn a lot from them, as they are, we once were, and as we are, they will become. What happens to most children when they hit the two year age mark? The story is that they become "terrible" and out of control. Why? Is it because for their entire lives to that point they have been "babied" and given everything they need to survive? I'm not saying this is bad; there is no way that I think we should leave an 18-month-old alone to fend for their self. I'm not saying that; I'm simply saying that we should look at this experience that all people share in and wonder. Maybe this stage of development has a correlation to the behavior of the people in the environment of the child. Maybe we breed a sense of entitlement in the children. They may simply be responding to our treatment. An interesting thought experiment. What is it that brings them out of the "terrible two's?" They become autonomous. The child starts learning to do things on their own. They can now tie their shoes, communicate their wants and needs with their parents through language, they can feed themselves with less help than before. Autonomy sets in and they act for themselves. Let's look back at ourselves. Are we autonomous when someone else is providing for our basic needs, such as food and shelter? Or are we reverting back to toddlerhood? Parens Patriae is the process of the state (or governing body) becoming the parent when a person (commonly a juvenile offender) is unable to care for their self and those responsible for them cannot do the job either - not necessarily the fault of anyone, it's just how it goes sometimes. The legislated parent then cares for the "child" and provides for their needs. Isn't this what is happening in the welfare system? People are unable, or unwilling, to do what is necessary to obtain resources to meet their basic needs (how do we define basic needs? This is a valid question; a question I don't feign to think I'm qualified to answer on my own) so someone else does it for them. The situation creates a parent-child dependency relationship. This relationship at first is good as it keeps the one who isn't able to provide for their self alive, just like the infant. After too long though, the one receiving the help becomes dependent and develops a sense of entitlement. Unless a rebirth of autonomy is being nurtured, the dependent will remain dependent upon the surrogate and the situation gets worse. Why does it happen this way? I don't know, nor do I know if it even does happen this way, but the analogy seems to fit, right? There must be intrinsic value in autonomy. Whether you believe it is a divinely given attribute of mankind, or a biologically developed attribute of an advanced organism, do you agree that autonomy appears to be valued by people? How many times have you heard someone you were teaching a skill say "I can do it!" with a bit of frustration? You hear it from preschoolers all the time. They want to do it. They want to show that they can do it. When does that sense of personal accomplishment run out? I don't want to point fingers or cast blame at people receiving welfare, not all of them, anyway. They are a product of a system, we all are products of a system, which has been tweaked and manipulated to create two separate parties, those with control and those being controlled. While we are the product and they have influenced us into the product we are, there is something innately special about the material we are comprised of. This product called the human being isn't like a wood or steel structure. This product has the ability to look at the hands which made it and say "No. I will not be what you've made me be." We can stop the production line and, well, change the formula. If we do, however, what keeps us from eventually tweaking and manipulating the formula ourselves?

Animals

I was writing a paper for my ethics class - which, by the way, I think philosophy is ridiculously useless - and the question of what gives value to people came up. The topic for writing had to do with God as the source of morality, basically. My thoughts brought me to thinking that the value of people is dependent in some way, or to some people, upon their (our) relationship with God. For those who believe in a God that is real and relates to people as Father to child, I assume they must see value in other people because they are children of God. At the very least, even if they don't see individual value in human life, they see value in their own relationship with God so they follow what he commands them to do, which includes treating other people well.

I come from the camp that believes all people are the children of God, thereby granting them intrinsic value. I wonder how I would value people if I didn't have this belief; I don't think that I can accurately suppose it as my beliefs are so much of who I am. Perhaps the value comes from a realization of what the self is. I would know how I value myself and then project that value upon other people. An interesting thing to think about. This next bit I will explore is heavily biased, which I don't apologize for, but I want to make it clear that I don't think this is how it is, it is just a route that my pondering took. It is a possible explanation from a strictly biological point of view, wherein humans are simply higher level organisms. It is interesting that I worry that my view might be offensive to someone who doesn't have the same core belief as me, when this approach may very well be what someone else's core belief is. All speculation of course, just another thought expansion exercise.

I suggest that the value of animal life is found in what value that life has for humans. The cow is only as valuable as the milk or meat it provides for humans. The goldfish is only as valuable as the aesthetic enjoyment it provides the child carrying it home in a plastic bag filled with water. A rat is as valuable as the fear it elicits when cast in a horror movie or the research done by inflicting it with disease in a laboratory. What does this animal do for me? That's the question to determine how much value its life is. If I think it will taste good or provide nutrition then I will kill it and eat it. If I think I can develop medicine to save people by subjecting the animal to life shortened by extreme suffering and disease, then OK. I'm not attempting to pass judgment on this approach, though the way I'm saying it certainly must exude some form of bias. I like to eat animals, and I am happy for medical research that is done to save human lives, so I guess I'm alright with this system. That's not the point; the point is that we seem to value animal life for what it can do for us. My question then is this; do we value human life for what it can do for us? If we do not value human life for being human life, or for the relationship between God and man, then is this how we value it?

Is the rich benefactor valued more highly than the beggar on the street because of what they can do for me, or because of some other reason? It could be said that we value hard work and accomplishment, so we value the rich benefactor more than the beggar because we attribute these to the rich benefactor more than the beggar. Have you noticed that I started this post by expressing my feeling that philosophy is ridiculous and useless, and then I proceeded to wax philosophical for the last few paragraphs? My logic was once described as schizophrenic; I do not disagree with that observation, not completely. Are people valued solely on what they can do for me or for the society I live in? It is a valid question. We readily kill and waste animals because what they do for us is more valuable than their existing in their own realm. Is this why some people readily kill and waste humans, because the death of a person is perceived as more valuable than the life of that person?

We objectify each other in so many ways. Consumerism is all about objectifying people. Is this bad? I vote for yes. It is bad when we put price tags on each other based on popular trends or on what we expect to get from them. Think about it for a minute, list the names or descriptions of the last ten people you came in contact with. Use a description if you didn't know the person, such as "store clerk" or "skateboarding on the sidewalk kid." Once you have the list, reorganize it from one to ten (with one being highest value and ten being lowest, or whatever, it's your list) in value order. Pretend you have to price these ten people for retail sale. How do you do it? Maybe I ought to do this little experiment myself, but I don't want to. Talking about it seems to suffice for me. If you stopped reading and did it, what did you learn? What aspects of the person did you, or would you, count valuable? What factors play in: how well you know them, how they treated you, what they looked like, what they were doing, etc? We make value judgments about people constantly. What are we using as the price guide for these judgments? That's what I'd like to know.

Let us suppose someone does the research and can say with statistical significance, "this is how people value other people." Then what? Does this information prove useful to us? I think it would be useful information as far as preventing some of the crimes (legislated, normative, moral or otherwise supposed as deviant) that result from objectification of people. These crimes are rampant and come in many forms. Various forms of abuse from physical to financial would fall into this category. I think genocide and slavery could be included as well. Perhaps with an understanding of how people value other people we could determine a better way to do it, and a way to teach that better way. I think if all of this was accomplished, we'd find that the answer lies in the teachings of Jesus Christ, which, simplified, says to treat others as you would have them treat you. Or, value people as you would have them value you. Hey! That's what we call the golden rule, Jesus taught that? Yes. Matthew 7:12 "Therefore all things whatsoever ye would that men should do to you, do ye even so to them..."

Well, this is already widely taught. Wc all learn it in kindergarten, we used to anyway. For some reason it doesn't stick with us. I don't know why it doesn't stick, but it sure doesn't seem to. Something else must come along and take precedence for our attention. I don't know what that is, could be any number of things. Maybe the answer to all of our problems between nations and within society could be found in finding what the distractions are and eliminating them. Good luck with that, right? Yeah, I'm going to watch TV now.

A Little Something I Had Typed Away Somewhere

I don't remember exactly when I typed this. It was saved in the documents folder on my laptop. I was perusing files to see what was saved in there and came across this and the blog is as good a place as any to say things like this, so here it is:

I like oatmeal cookies with chocolate chips. Raisins are good too, but you can never go wrong with chocolate chips. I also like pancakes with chocolate chips in them. Pancakes are one of my most favorite foods. I also like to eat oatmeal. It’s a natural process then to try chocolate chips in oatmeal. I did that this morning. I poured a handful of semi-sweet chips into the steaming bowl of oatmeal. The chocolate promptly melted as I stirred them in. It looked like something that might taste OK, but it had a funny taste to it. After adding an unhealthy amount of sugar, the funny taste faded. It always amazes me how I think about something and then do it, only to have an unexpected result, which upon further pondering seems so obvious I begin to question how I didn't expect it from the start. I honestly thought the chocolate chips would maintain their shape and not just melt into the shapeless goo that is oatmeal. After all, raisins don't melt (but they do rehydrate a bit, which is neat).

Driver Safety Folks are Hating on Texting, Why Not Ajax, Too?

The text message: a useful tool of communication or a detriment to relationship building? There used to be a time when you would hear the statement "he dumped her over the phone!" Now you hear the same incredulity of voice, but the statement is slightly altered, "he dumped her through a text!" I guess there used to be a day when people took care of relationship business in person, face to face. It makes sense that once the technology was available to avoid an awkward or difficult situation that it was utilized for that purpose. Then once you are taking care of such affairs with a phone conversation, why not escape further into the text-generation of avoidance?

If you have heard the statements above and have agreed with the surprise of the situation, why were you surprised? Is there something abnormal about breaking off a relationship over the phone or through a text message? From what I've heard from people there is. "The least they could do is say it to my face." Well, no, the least they could do would be to forget they know you and ignore your existence, so maybe you should be happy that you got the phone call or text. I don't mean to be rude, I do think that certain aspects of relationships ought to be conducted in person, but is it morally wrong not to? That is a question for people with more time to waste than me, not for someone smarter, just someone who has more time to waste (some philosophical questions are less useful than baseball cards in the spokes of a motorcycle). I digress.

Breaking up using a phone is only a part of a larger issue. It is an example of a relationship interaction that might be best performed face to face. Personally, I like text messages. I think they are convenient sometimes (especially when you want to avoid a lengthy phone conversation or face to face meeting) and it is fun at other times. Sometimes you just need to say how much you like Lucky Charms, but that's all you have to say. Other times you'll be late, but you don't want to say it, it's easier to just send a message. And sometimes it is easiest to text a conversation because you are able to avoid awkward and difficult situations. I don't think that is the best way to do it, but it is easier, and human nature says to take the path of least resistance.

Text messaging is great between friends and family with established relationships or with new acquaintances when the subject matter is neutral or inane. Why? Because it is a very impersonal form of communication and does not support healthy relationship building or growth. Not all forms of communication are created equal. When we talk to each other, there is so much more than just what we say that is involved. Body language and vocal inflection are just as loud as the words we choose. The speaker speaks with more than just their mouth, and the listener listens with more than just their ears. When you take a conversation to the phone, you eliminate all but the voice and hearing. One step further (away) is the text message where you lose all body language and vocal inflection. You also lose the spontaneity of word selection. A text message can be minutes or hours in the creation, allowing a person to carefully craft what they say. This adds a new element to the mix, not necessarily a good element. There is definitely some loss in a text message conversation, or a habitual series of text messages throughout the day between two people, at least in comparison to face to face conversation.

This is why I think that building a relationship on text messaging is so dangerous. I have done it and I have seen other people do it. You meet someone (I'm talking dating relationships specifically) and you are interested in them. You start the process of spending time together, but then you introduce text messaging. You might think this is a great way to get to know each other. You are able to have a constant conversation throughout a day - even though schedules prevent you from being together. It is my opinion that texting in this way does not build a stable relationship. I will concede that it doesn't have to hurt a healthy relationship, but I think that it does pose a real danger, especially to the superficial relationship (meaning "when Hollister Co. girl meets frat boy").

This isn't a hard and fast rule of course, I'm just a guy speculating based on things I've done, seen, and heard. I feel confident in declaring that intimacy is crucial to every relationship that wants to be healthy, romantic or otherwise. Being close with people, having a foundation and expectation of trust and honesty, is imperative to success. Not only honesty in what you say, but in how you present yourself. Texting doesn't lend to honesty, face to face does. It is so much easier to misrepresent yourself when not in person. This doesn't mean bold lies, but just warping reality to take less away from your ego and make you seem better than you are. People typically do this anyway, but it is easier to get away with through text messages. As I said before, "A text message can be minutes or hours in the creation, allowing a person to carefully craft what they say" (Ajax, 2010). Does APA provide a format for citing yourself within the very same document?

Intimacy is to be closely acquainted. Pop-culture these days links it with sex, but that is just another sign of the degraded nature of society. Any relationship can involve intimacy; if it is an important relationship, it probably should. In my book, sincerity is the primary step towards intimacy. Being sincere with people provides opportunity for them to develop trust for you. When they trust you they will include you in more areas of their life, such as the daily struggles and achievements. They will come to you for help, comfort, and to share joy. These are the hallmarks of healthy dating relationship foundations. Sincerity is best expressed in person and trust is best established in the same manner. Text messages are too ambiguous, for reasons mentioned earlier, and they don't say "I really care." Now, I'm not saying that face to face is the only way to express care behind your words, in some situations a phone call is more practical, but texting just doesn't do it.

The early days of a relationship bring so many unknown situations and conversations which are meant to find out information. This information includes the outward expressions of personality – hobbies, interests, etc. – as well as the inner workings of personality. Yes, a text message can deliver, with much success, a conversation of Q: what's your favorite food? A: pizza. Think about that for a minute. Think about some other questions that would work: What's your favorite movie? Do you like sports? What is your favorite band? And so on. Do these questions reveal anything about the person? Do these questions have the potential to reveal anything about the person with how they are answered? What about questions regarding the person's family, or friends? How much might you miss out on if these fun fact questions are all determined through text messaging?

You now want to ask: does it have to be one way or the other? Does texting destroy a relationship before it can get started? I respond: of course it doesn't. Then what is the point? The point is that we as a society are withdrawing from others at an alarming rate. Every few months you look up and some other menial task is automated. Life keeps getting easier and easier, right? Machines do our heavy lifting and some of the dangerous jobs. Computers figure things out faster than people do. With all of the luxuries we enjoy, with all of the non-human entities doing our jobs for us, shouldn't we be prospering and having more fulfilling lives? Shouldn't we be able to take care of each other better? Perhaps time was never the issue. We never were too busy providing for ourselves to take care of each other; we were simply too busy caring about ourselves to take care of each other.

Texting isn't inherently selfish or a direct representation of man's indifference to his fellow man, but there is correlation. Why don't we help each other more? We don't care about each other enough. Why don't we care about each other enough? We have distanced ourselves and created walls. The less we see each other the easier it is to ignore each other. The less we talk to each other, the same result. I suppose there is some irony in the path my thoughts have taken when considering the method I am using to communicate them. Text messaging isn't immoral, but it isn't real, either. Real conversation provides opportunity to express sincerity. Sincerity provides opportunity to develop trust. Trust leads to care and care to support. I don't know what the bottom line is, but I recommend building relationships in person.

My Thoughts on "Us and Them" Mentality...and What Follows

I've been thinking about this topic for a while now. Last semester I had a class on criminal corrections in which I began thinking about the topic in this way. I also had a U.S. history class and the idea seemed relevant there while discussing slavery in antebellum America. Currently, I am in an abnormal psychology class and the idea recurs while reviewing the diagnosing and labeling processes that go with mental health issues. In each case there is a situation of "us" vs. "them." I'd say it is a clearly defined issue of "us" and "them," but I don't think there is anything clear about it. Some definitions may be appropriate at this point (definitions which I am defining from my own mind, no direct reference to anything, just a compilation of ideas from all that I've learned recently).

The Us perception of Us

We are something special. We are not capable of devious, underhanded, criminal or un-virtuous behavior. We are the moral superior. We are in control of all of our thoughts and actions. We know what is right and we never deviate from it.

The Us perception of Them

They are immoral, dirty minded, shiftless, lazy and godless. They are sick and twisted in their actions, only surpassed in their deviance by their actions. They are victims of their sensual nature. They are different than us; different in upbringing or something, but just plain different. They are all that is wrong with society, a plague to all of us.

My own personal perception of Us

We are them.

My own personal perception of Them

They are us.

What do I mean by that? Are we all simultaneously capable of deviousness and virtuousness? Are we in control of our thoughts and actions, as well as subject to our base desires? Yes. Emphatically yes. There is nothing done by one person that cannot be done by another. We all have the capacity for amazing creation or awesome destruction. The failure to realize this dichotomy may be one explanation for some of the troubles we see in society today.

The reason this is a problem is that when we view other people as them, and seek comfort in being part of us, we create a deep-set separation between each other. If they are over there, they can't be over here. If they can't be over here, then we must not be the same. If we are not the same, and I am good, then they must be bad. If they are bad, they don't deserve the same things which I, being good, deserve. If I am human, they must be something less.

Slavery in America thrived on the development of the idea that one person was not on the same level as another and could therefore justly be managed by the other. This difference of level was been based on race, but it could be based on ethnicity or other reasons, such as birth, in some countries which operate on a caste system. By dehumanizing someone and putting them on a lower level than ourselves we are able to justify our actions and thoughts against them. Perhaps justify isn't the right word, maybe rationalize? Yes, I think that is better. If you are actually rational about it, can you really believe that humans have separate levels that condone slavery?

In the case of slavery, we aren't differentiating between us and them to protect ourselves from them, but rather to protect, or defend, our actions towards them. But in the case of criminals, we are differentiating to protect ourselves from danger, or are we? Perhaps we are protecting our delicate self-perceptions. Just last week I read in the news about a man in China who entered a kindergarten and began attacking children and teachers with a knife. Twenty eight children were injured. My first thought, 'what is wrong with that guy?' A valid question, something is wrong, but it isn't that he is one of them and not one of us. I don't know what happened to the man to lead him to such behavior. I don't know what his life has been like to lead him to the point where he would make the decision to turn a knife on children. I don't know why, but I know that he is a human the same as I am a human. The difference isn't in what he and I are, but rather what he and I are becoming.

Becoming is the process of living. This is the process of creating or destroying. The man in China, the kids who bring guns to school, Adolf Hitler and me; what do we have in common? We have the same human capacity to create or to destroy. It seems out of place to put my name in a grouping such as that, but at the most basic level, it is a legitimate grouping, as it would be if your name was added as well. The “us and them” way of thinking prevents this grouping from occurring and makes “us” think that we are above such a distinction. Many philosophers and theorizers have written about the need to accept our "dark side," not to cater to it, but to be aware of it. The danger isn’t in admitting that we have capacity to destroy, but it is in denying it. When we let ourselves be aware of our capacity, and then promote the good and control the bad, we are becoming.

This is not a quick or easy process in anyway. It is a day to day battle. What we conquered yesterday might come back to fight again three months down the road after a stressful situation or triggering event. Our brains remember everything, though we are not always able to recall every detail, it is there and can be recalled given the right circumstances. Though it may sound hopeless and futile to attempt control, it is not. If it were, we would be seeing a lot more of the destructive forces in life. At times it seems we are surrounded by destruction because that is what the media focuses on. Probably because it is emotional and it speaks to us, as we all have that destructive side of nature. Maybe that is why we like movies about things we would never really do in life, we can relate to it somehow. Most of us don't do it in real life. Most of us rise above the circumstances of life and control our duality. Most of us are in the becoming phase in which we embrace creation and control destruction. Control is the key word in my opinion. Denial of a very real part of ourselves leads to lashing out in the way we are trying to avoid. Sort of like a pendulum, it only swings so far in one direction before it swings violently back in the other.

Control doesn't mean that we embrace our destructive nature and let parts of it come out to play occasionally. For example, other people have murdered, so I must have the capacity to murder as well. Control doesn't mean I physically attack people, but not to death. Control means recognizing the potential I have to do harm and what situations might encourage that potential in me. Then, I become aware of my thoughts and behavior in those situations. I allow myself to process thoughts and reactions, but I have to keep my perspective focused on the process of becoming. It is at this point in this thought exercise that I realize I don't know of any practical way to do this. I guess this is where my observations stop for now.

For the obligatory wrap-up I'll just say that I think it is very important for us to recognize that we all have the capacity for whatever good or bad we have seen other people do. How we measure ourselves ought to be in the process of becoming (promoting creation and controlling destruction) rather than denying. There is no "us and them," we are all us, and them. "We" will never solve the world's problems; you and I have to do it individually. We are a collective of individuals.

Ajax is in Bad Shape

It is 12:00 am on the button as I type this. I'll be posting it later, so I guess it doesn't matter when I type it, or post it for that matter. Needless to say, I will be posting it. I will digress to discuss this phrase, "needless to say." I heard a doosie today. I love when people misuse this phrase. Before that though, just the phrase itself is pretty ridiculous, the mime of literary idioms if you will. "If you will" is another good one, maybe it can be the clown-car gag of literary idioms. Basically "if you will" is just for people who want to make their writing sound snootier, which is why I use it. But "needless to say," well, if it was really unnecessary to be said, then why are you saying it? It is either an affront to the intelligence of the audience, as in, "I shouldn't need to say this, but I did notice your knuckles dragging while you approached me, so…" or it falls into the category of trying to enhance the appeal of your communication. I can't just say, "The kids went crazy after the football game and three of them wound up being arrested." I'd have to say "The kids went crazy after the football game and, needless to say, three of them wound up being arrested." That doesn't really seem "enhanced." I guess I'm going to change my statement to "the only reason to use 'needless to say' is to imply that your audience is in the cognitive slow lane." There is intrinsic laughability in the phrase being used at any time, but the best is when it is used improperly, such as, "well, the dog has been chewing up everything in sight, and I mean EVERYTHING. Then add in the attack on the mailman, and they say that once a dog tastes human blood, well…you know. So when the neighbor asked if I'd watch their 2-year-old, I was pretty nervous. Needless to say, everything was fine." Needless to say?! No, I think it was very needful to say. If you are leading up to a certain conclusion you can't just throw in a needless to say and then turn the story around, it doesn't make sense. Anyway, I heard a good one of those kinds today and was just thinking about it a little.

End of the digression. It is midnight. Recently my roommates and I have been doing a lot of talking about getting some exercise going. As the title states, Ajax is in bad shape. This goes back to my joke about trying to save some money, you know, tightening the belt, so I quit going to the gym. Well, my pants are getting tighter, just a bit. What can you do when Ben and Jerry's is on sale for $2.30 a pint. I'd be wrong not to buy several. And then Oreo cookies, well, you gotta have those! Needless to say (checkmate!), I need to get back to the gym. This is the way our conversations have been going lately. It got really funny yesterday when one of my roommates was talking to a mutual friend and then I had dinner with her last night and I was talking about my plan to exercise again and she said that my roommate had just been talking about that too. It was funny to me and him anyway. I don't think that is proper grammar. I'm not worried about grammar though, I'm worried about my cholesterol and this little stomacher I've got developing. If this was 1770's Philadelphia it wouldn't be a problem. You know the rest. You see, I want to develop a Brad Pitt type appearance. He's a good looking fellow. Right now I'm on a young-Steve-Buscemi plateau. Nothing against Buscemi, he's a funny guy, but he's no Brad Pitt. Ben and Jerry aren't going to help me get to where I'd like to be, I know that, yet I continue to sit all day and eat ice cream. Until tonight. My roommates decided to start running. They've done their run once so far and invited me tonight. Usually I'm in bed earlier and get up earlier, but lately I've been letting that schedule slip back. When they said run at 11:30 pm, I said OK.

Here is the run: about 2 blocks to the gas station to buy soda and energy drinks (The energy drinks are so they can stay up all night to watch the World Cup broadcast from South Africa). Let me tell you, or, needless to say, it was pretty funny that we ran for about 4 minutes and then they bought 40 oz. sodas. I bought a Gatorade. I at least wanted to look like I was trying. We get out of the store and start jogging again, but we couldn't stop laughing. There we were - me with a Gatorade, each of them with a 40 oz. soda and one with a bag of energy drinks. Shuffling/jogging along, at break-neck speeds…yeah. It must have been some sight for the passing motorists: three young guys in exercise apparel, jogging along with huge soda cups in hand. Kind of like the folks ordering a diet soda at KFC (I know, diet soda is blah blah blah and just because blah blah blah. Whatever, it's an easy joke to make, so I made it. You laughed, even if only slightly, and even if only subconsciously).

I don't know if what I've typed here has done justice to the experience I just had, but it had to be said. Our little expedition took all of 20 minutes and covered 4 blocks. The first thing I did after getting back to the apartment? Eat a cookie. A tragic tale? Perhaps, but you've gotta start somewhere. In my defense, it was a peanut butter cookie; I hear protein is good to eat after exercising. There's still protein in peanut butter cookies, right?

A Day at the Races

I typed this up at midnight last night, or this morning, whichever you prefer. Sometimes I'll have a thought while lying in bed waiting for sleep to overtake me. That sounds so dramatic, that's why I typed it that way instead of just saying "waiting to fall asleep." Good, huh? So I get these ideas and sometimes I just entertain them in my head, figuratively writing out a masterful essay or comedy routine. Those become lost to the ages. Other times I'll type a note in my phone or scribble a note down using my phone as a light. This time I actually turned my computer on and waited forever for the three-year-old slowpoke to boot up. Then I typed the following:

Some people say that the first step in a race is the hardest one to take. This is because that first step represents weeks, months or even years of commitment and preparation. It is the culmination of early morning runs, muscle strain, dehydration, sunburn, windburn, trips and falls, blisters and miles and miles of being out of breath. The right diet, the right coaches, the right practice routines and nothing else. Everything in preparation for that one step; certainly there is a lot that goes into it. Moments before the race begins you are lined up with others who have similarly sacrificed and prepared. You focus and wait for the preparatory remarks. At the sound of the starter's pistol your muscles contract and spring into action, your first foot crosses the line and the race has begun. The hardest step has been taken. This is what some people say, but not me.

This is the easiest step to take. You don't even have to be in the race to take it. Any fool, completely oblivious to his surroundings, could stumble upon the starting line while his sights are set on the cheese-steak hut on the infield. All he wants is a sandwich and he is going to get one. In his tunnel vision he walks right onto the track, the pistol goes off; he is nudged by you – who just lost the race you've spent three months preparing for by bumping into the guy – and takes a stumble step to the side, crossing the starting line. He started the race, quicker than you did I might add, without a day of preparation. That doesn't sound like the hardest step to me. I'd suppose that the last step is the hardest with all of its symbolism of enduring the pain and exhaustion which accompanies a race, but that won't do either.

The runner whose spleen ruptures three feet before the finish line and stumbles the last bit before collapsing just over the line has still finished the race. While that last step might have been excruciatingly painful, it wasn't difficult, it was just collapsing. Perhaps, relatively speaking, the final step is even easier than the first step. It won't do to say that the final step is the hardest step. Maybe there isn't any hardest step. Maybe the hardest part of a race is trying to keep in your lane or stay on the designated race route. Maybe avoiding collisions (remember that one with the cheese-steak enthusiast at the starting line?) with other runners is the hardest part. Maybe the hardest part is when something inside your midsection starts to cramp up and you get a Charlie horse and your smooth, elliptical-machine-stride downgrades to a wounded-elk-running-on-marbles gallop. The hardest part is keeping the desired end in mind. Maybe this isn't true for you, but it is for me. Starting and finishing have their flare and pomp, but maintaining focus is the real feat in my book. I start and finish things every day. I usually start more than I finish though.

As I said, I think starting is an easy task. Somewhere along the line I get distracted or disgruntled or disenfranchised or disinterested or just plain diss'd by a homie. It is easy to lose focus on the desired end when it is raining on your camping trip and you don't have any rain gear. Waking up in a cold puddle or finding yourself in the wounded-elk-running-on-marbles gallop can be very debilitating on your end result orientation. That's why I think keeping that focus and continuing to run is the hardest part of the race.

A Pertinent Question of Life

I had three classes today. Each one frustrated me in its own special way. I won't get into the details, but suffice it to say I was tired of it all when I was done with the last one. Happily, on my way out of class I ran into a friend. We spent almost an hour talking. I explained to him my frustration and we discussed that, along with everything else in life. It was one of those deeply intellectual conversations, and as much as I don't care for philosophy, it had plenty of that as well. I like to philosophize in so far as I like to think about things, critically. Philosophy fails in that it is useless. A definition my friend gave that he heard from someone was that as soon as philosophy is applied it ceases to exist. My question to that is what good is it then? What good is talking and thinking if it leads you to doing, but then you never do? It is no good at all. Thinking about saving a person from a river, running to the bank with rope in hand and then just standing there doesn't help the person (maybe it gives the drowning person a false glimmer of hope before they sink beneath the water and their lungs fill with water, so I guess it isn't fair to say you aren't doing anything, just not anything beneficial). You help yourself though. You are all ready to attempt a rescue of the person, but instead you do nothing and keep your shoes dry. Philosophy not applied is keeping your shoes dry and letting a person drown.

Well, we had a long discussion and debate over lots of topics. We worked through some ideas and each said our part. To me it was more beneficial than the class I had just taken because my friend and I discussed and found resolution. I walked away with a different way of thinking. Whether or not I remember this change and I use it to change my behavior is another story. Our conversation was useless if I don't change. Just a lot of gum-flapping and lung compressions. Just a lot of philosophy. But, if he and I walk away and give those ideas some more thought, and change how we interact with other people and how we think for ourselves, then something good comes of it. If we apply what we discussed. I guess I am too harsh on my classes that I label as being useless and just a lot of hot air. Some of the other students probably are invested in the classes more than I am, I hope they are. For them the classes are as beneficial as my conversation in the hall was to me. I'm too quick to judge the situation from my point of view. I need to be aware of other sides. Not necessarily to give up what I perceive, but to be aware and hopefully really understand a situation.

I don't want to get into the details of my frustrations (I've already vented enough) or the content of the conversation, but I did walk away with one question that I want to mention. My friend posed the question of whether we respect the law or the law giver most. In the context it was of a religious nature; do we follow God or do we follow His laws? I think this question can give anyone enough to ponder about, whether you are religious or not. In any instance, do you respect the creator or their creation? This is the question I walked away pondering today. I don't think it is a new question, I've probably asked myself this question countless times in different ways. Today it has some direct meaning to me and I think it gives me a lot to think about. I can use this question to improve myself. It has direct influence on my motivation and intent behind everything I think and do, it could anyway. I hope that I will let it. I hope that I will make something meaningful come from the conversation I had. If I don't then I'm just raging against the machine, a machine that I am part of and regularly perform maintenance on.

To Have and Have Not

Today is the final day of regular classes for my undergraduate experience. I am pleased. If you have read my post previous to this you will have a glimpse of how the impending graduation is affecting me. For a week or two my creativity and intelligence factors have seemingly been less than what they usually are. Rereading that last sentence makes me think the drought isn't fully recompensed yet. Moving on. The reading assignment for today's ethics class was a New York Times (1999) article, "The Singer Solution to World Poverty" by Peter Singer. It is an interesting piece, so I would like to comment on it here. In a way it is my swan song after a final semester of complacency and just getting by academically. Formal schooling doesn't have a monopoly on learning; it doesn't even have a Baltic Ave on learning. [Which reminds me; a long time ago I mentioned an article I was writing about formal education, I will perhaps return to that writing after school is over.]

Peter Singer is a professor at Princeton University, and a crusader for helping the world's impoverished, and animals. He is utilitarian and relativistic in his personal ethics, from what I can find written about him online. Apparently he is quite a controversial thinker. I don't know about all of that, though, perhaps I will read more about him later. I want to comment on the "World Poverty" article. Singer sets up a scenario to support his argument, which I will explain after I explain the scenario.

A man nearing retirement age invests his money in an expensive car with appreciating value - making it a true investment. This man enjoys using his car as much as he enjoys keeping it as his retirement account. One day he parks by a railway and takes a walk. He notices a runaway train, with no passengers or operators, on course to collide with a child. The child is too far from the man for him to affect any successful rescue attempt, except for throwing a switch and diverting the train to another track. Well what's the problem? The only way to save the child is to throw the switch and divert the train? Do it. Unfortunately for the man, his car is parked on the side rail and will be destroyed if he diverts the train. He has a choice to make, save the child and lose his retirement fund, or let the child (who he doesn't know and has zero conscious attachment to) die and save his retirement. You probably have an immediate emotional response to this scenario, keep that in mind.

People spend more money than they need to, those who have money to spend, that is. After necessities are paid for, what do we do with our money? Singer suggests that it is immoral not to use our excess for the benefit of other people throughout the world. In the retirement investor example, the man has to decide between his personal well-being and the life of another person. This is analogous to all of us. Money spent on convenience food and HD television could be better spent on saving a starving child, vaccinating an at-risk village in a developing nation or literating (my word) the illiterate of the world. These examples are mine, but the message is Singer's. Those who have ought to give to those who have not. When I buy the $800 guitar instead of the equally playable $200 one, I am neglecting the child on the train track to save my expensive car. And I am acting immorally by doing so, per Singer.

I agree with Singer, in principle, but I don't know where the line ought to be drawn. How do we determine how much to give? I can certainly cut back on some of my luxury spending in order to donate more to charity, but when you put it in terms like the train track scenario, how much more could I cut back in order to save more children? What if there are three tracks to choose between switching to and each has a child on it? Maybe I have time to drive my car in front of the train to stop it and save all of the children, but I only have enough time to get on the track with the car, not get out. How far do I go in sacrificing for the starving children of the world? Do I give my life for them?

There are probably sufficient resources for all people in the world to live comfortably, so why do we have such stratification? I suggest that the answer can be found in the first of the Ten Commandments of the Old Testament. Exodus 20:3 "Thou shalt have no other gods before me." It isn't a matter of money or resources, but a matter of focus. Are we focused on accumulating goods because they make us feel good? What other purpose is there for collecting things? I think we all have the tendency to want to feel good, it is a natural drive. "Feeling good" can be defined and expressed in many different ways, of course. And we all pursue different avenues to reach that destination. Singer addresses one aspect of that in what he calls luxuries, categorized by things acquired beyond what would be termed a necessity. It is very subjective, but I think we can agree that we all do things seeking to feel good, or at least better than we previously were feeling.

I don't want to whittle this down into one form or another of ethical philosophy, meaning a concrete reason why people "do" or "don't." I simply think that there is an individual motivation in most, if not all, people saying "I want to feel good, or at least better than I do now." I'm not making implications about whether or not this is right or how it ought to be, it just is. So, we seek to feel good and focus on that. Unless we seek to feel good through obtaining a steady influence of the love of God in our lives, our focus isn't going to be on God.

The first commandment says that we should have no other gods before our God, our Heavenly Father. This means that we are to put no other thing, person or ideal above our focus on God. He promises that if we trust in him and exercise faith he will provide for us. Jesus posed to his disciples, "...Consider the lilies of the field, how they grow; they toil not, neither do they spin: And yet I say unto you, that even Solomon in all his glory was not arrayed like one of these" (Matthew 6:28-29). OK, now tie it all together, Ajax.

Singer suggests we meet our needs and then give of our excess to help others. Many of us, upon hearing that, start hemming and hawing (whatever that means) about "what is a need?" or "doesn't God want us to be happy and doesn't buying a nicer car make me happy?" How about "but I work hard for my money, can't I spend it how I want. Let the starving people work hard for themselves." These are excuses and rationalizations. The issue being addressed by Singer is superficial. Sharing our excess resources is good, but it is akin to treating symptoms and not addressing underlying causes. Will an increase in charitable donations bring about improved living conditions for some? I believe it would. But it won't fix the problem. In fact, it could make things worse. Something for nothing does nothing good for everyone.

What I want to derive out of all of this, finally, is that we need to change our focus. Singer addresses a problem using money as the surface feature, but structurally it is a matter of focus. The man in the fancy car scenario is focused on himself more than the life of a child. He would rather allow a child to die (by the way, in the scenario presented by

Singer the man does let the child die to protect his car) than to sacrifice his material goods. It isn't a matter simply of money, but of focus. Why do we spend our money on extravagances and luxuries rather than use our resources to help others? Because our focus is on the self.

When I read the article by Singer I felt a twinge of pain, knowing that I indulge in excess. Can I be more charitable, sure, but a more important matter is where I fix my focus. I think it comes down to a question such as this "what do I want in (or from) life?" When we honestly address this question and take some time to think about how we can obtain what we want I think we can begin to address the structure behind the issue presented by Singer. Am I in this for myself? For my family? For God? What do I want, how can I get it? But even if everyone took a moment to contemplate and evaluate their motivations we wouldn't see universal solution to problems like poverty. Some people would still decide their focus should be self, and would continue to act as such. Does that mean we don't bother? I don't think so. I know I can't change much. Perhaps I can't change anything other than myself, but I can change myself. If I can reassess my life and fix my focus then I think I'm doing okay.

So I try. I think and plan and remember, for a little while. Then I get home to my TV, Internet connected computer, refrigerator full of convenience food and other such amenities, and I slowly forget the starving children and my human connection with them. I forget God and return to self-focus. Until another instance of bringing these things to my mind and I feel guilty and desire to better align my focus and improve. It is a process. Sometimes you've gotta break the machine and rebuild. Once the robot starts laser-blasting people with its eyes and snapping necks, do you just wring your hands and lament over ever making the robot, but decide there is nothing you can do now because it is already in motion? NO! (Hopefully) You dismantle the robot and rebuild it. Sometimes you have to dismantle your life and rebuild it. It is a process.

In my personal revolution I sometimes have these moments when I realize I need to dismantle the machine and start over. And with each new build the machine works better than it did before.

The Root Cause

We discussed problem solving in my cognitive psychology class. Getting at the root cause was one technique or formula or something. I admit, I don't pay attention in class. No qualifiers for that statement, I just don't do it. Anyhow, I remember root cause being written on the chalk board. And now I will explain the root cause to our countries problems (analogously, and in a make-believe way). As I sat at our kitchen table this evening eating bacon and cheddar flavored cheese from a can, with crackers, a beam of light shined down and inspired me. The cause to all of our problems is processed cheese in a pressurized can that doesn't need refrigeration. There are three issues here: 1. processed cheese 2. pressurized can 2. plus 1, meaning 3. (I typed 2 instead of 3 and just ran with it) doesn't need refrigeration.

Processed Cheese

This is a problem because it represents how far from natural we have gotten. Our lives are full of counterfeit attempts at reality. Just turn on *MTV* or any of the network channels during prime-time. Reality is *Facebook* and television? For some of us it is, maybe not all of the time, but more than we might realize. There were once ideas that some characteristics, virtues and rules/laws were natural. There were rights that were free by virtue of being a human. People didn't need to pay for water or for air. Folks were free to pursue their interests and industry. For the most part we still can, but I think it is sometimes helpful to look at the direction rather than the location. Are we on an upward, downward or neutral slope? The point is that everything is processed, or forced, or legislated.

Processed cheese is an amalgamation of other types of cheese, created specifically for its "manipulatable" qualities. It is an interesting connection for us "paranoid" types to make about life these days. With an over-encroaching government (in my opinion) it seems that we are becoming processed cheese. Look it up. Head over to *Wikipedia* and read about processed cheese and its advantages. See if you can draw some similarities between the stuff and what's going on in the U.S. these days. What reality are you living in? There was once a great deal of importance put on "natural" and "unalienable" and "basic," and now there seems to be a swing of the pendulum over to "processed" and "dependent" and "bureaucracy."

Pressurized Can

There is a warning on the side of the cheese can which says to be careful because the contents are under pressure. Along with our being processed, we are lazy. Does it get lazier than receiving cheese from a can with no more than a slight press on the nozzle? A sharp cheddar I.V. drip is the only way I could think of making it easier. Maybe that's the next breakthrough in junk food. There once was a time when people had to work to eat. They *had* to. If they didn't work then they didn't eat. There are still many people who embrace that principle, but there are some who would rather whine, protest and elect corrupt people into government office for their food than to work for it. Getting something for nothing, especially the "essentials" is not good for people. I'm not anti-gift giving, quite the opposite, I love giving things to people, but continuously receiving something for nothing creates dependency. Look at all of the Hollywood stars gone bad. Something for nothing leads to entitlement which leads to dependency. If I don't have to work for it I begin to lift myself up and think that I am deserving of the handout. Then I expect it and if I don't get it I become a little stinker. Eventually, my ability to be self-sufficient, my autonomy, atrophies and I become dependent on the giver.

A can of pressurized cheese isn't evil. I am using it as a means to an end in describing how I think that tendency towards "something for nothing," as well as laziness, is one of our major problems in the world today.

Doesn't Need Refrigeration

This is where the analogy gets deeper. Or, sounds more like I'm contradicting myself. In point one I suggested that we have strayed from natural, which is bad. I am now going to say that natural, when left alone, becomes corrupted. Cheese, left without refrigeration becomes corrupted; not that it participates in shady deals with people who have criminal tendencies, but rather it spoils so that you don't want to eat it. I just said natural is the state we want, but now I'm saying that natural isn't self-sustaining. Stick with me. Cheese needs to be refrigerated, but cheese in a can doesn't. The cheese in the can has been manipulated so far from its natural state (ignore that cheese is milk manipulated from *its* natural state. We aren't adding that into this analogy) that it no longer is in danger of going bad without refrigeration. Perhaps it isn't even cheese any more. That's what I'm trying to get at, without the need for refrigeration you no longer have cheese. How is this representative of a problem we see in the world today? Without God people are no longer people, not in their truest form. I believe we need God to survive well. Many people survive, but do they survive well? Again, a very subjective matter to discuss. I'll keep it simple (if that is still possible): real cheese without refrigeration will spoil; real people without God will spoil.

The forces that processed the cheese, put it under pressure, and made it not need refrigeration are like the forces that are processing us, making us not want to work and leading us away from God. I'm not saying that *Kraft Foods* is out to destroy us; at least, I can't confirm that they are or are not. I am saying that while I was eating cheese from a can, bacon flavored cheese at that, I realized that there are some similarities between cheese and people. And maybe that means something.

This account is farce, but with underlying ideas to think about, as disjointed as they may be. I am living a personal revolution. There are two primary uses of the word revolution: an orbit around a fixed point and a process of changing power or control structure (paraphrased from the *American Heritage Dictionary* and *Wikipedia*, respectively). I would say that my personal revolution is attempting to fit both definitions. I am trying to change my personal power struggle with myself as well as correct my orbit around a fixed point. Perhaps I can use the example of cheese in a can to help me accomplish my revolution.

Don't Drink the Water

Imagine we are all together in a body of water. The water is our connection with each other. If someone contaminates the water, everyone suffers, even the one doing the contamination. With this scenario it makes sense that the person doing the contaminating will not do it for long as it has adverse impact on them as well. Now imagine that a boat is floating by. If someone gets into that boat he is no longer connected to us through the water. Now if someone contaminates the water, all but the one in the boat is affected. What if the one in the boat does the contaminating? He doesn't have to deal with the contamination while he is sitting safely in his ship. He does have a personal connection with the people in the water though, as he was once there with them. Also, he might have a moral code preventing him from doing harm to others.

Let's suppose he has the means to contaminate the water, but decides not to. But what if someone else is in the boat and this other person wants the water contaminated? The man from the water has two options, contaminate or don't. The second man begins to offer the man from the water all kinds of things that he likes. Eventually, the man from the water gives in and begins contaminating the water. Now all of the people he used to be connected with begin to suffer, while he enjoys his new gifts with the second man in the boat.

Imagine a country founded on principles of self-governance. The people of this country saw the benefit for a controlling body to protect those with less power, while not losing the ideal of self-governance. The governing body would be made up of the people in the water. They wouldn't go sit in boats; they would stay in the water. The governors and the governed would all be one people. Should a person decide to contaminate, the governors would intervene for the good of the community. Should the governors decided to contaminate, the people would intervene for the good of the community. In any case, everyone was in the water together, contamination from one affected all. Eventually, the governors decided they could do a better job from the boat, so they climbed aboard. For a while they were able to remember the people they used to associate with in the water. They kept the water clean, even from the boat. But all along there was a man in the boat, riding along. He began to offer certain privileges and gifts for the governors to go against their promises to the people. Some gave way, then others, until they all were participating in the contamination. They didn't suffer from within the walls of their boat, but the people in the water did.

You are What I Think You Are and I Am What You Think I Am

For my ethics class homework I read a chapter about relativism: cultural and subjective. The writing portion of the assignment was to speak to whether or not we agree with these theories and why. While I believe that there are objective rules of morality, I don't believe that *I* can tell anyone else that they are *objective* and expect them to take my word for it. I agree with relativism. There is no way that any person can prove objectivism. If there is I don't know about it. That's not saying much; there is certainly a lot that I don't know about. But I've been through enough classes where this topic has been discussed and there isn't any moral objectivity for proof. There is subjectivity which leads to a belief in objectivity. That is my suggestion.

I believe in a personal God...personal to everyone. His laws are objective, that is, they apply equally to all people. I believe this. I also believe that his justice in upholding the law incorporates mercy, making the law just for all people, while maintaining objectivity. We are all accountable for the law, but culpable only to the extent which we are capable. A decision that no earthly tribunal can make. It is up to God. I believe this to be objective, but I believe it because of subjective experience. It is impossible for me to prove that what I believe is the case for everyone, or for anyone. It is an individual task that must be accomplished dependent upon the individual's desire and interest. It is subjective. This is why I believe that moral rules can only be discussed in subjective terms among people, unless there has been similar subjective experience which leads to the acceptance of divine objectivity.

Murder is immoral because a collective body of individuals says so (cultural relativism), because an individual says so (subjective relativism) or because God - possibly through a prophet - says so (objective). I, personally, me, Ajax, cannot prove the objective morality of life, but a group of people can band together and establish a rule for themselves. In my opinion this establishes relativism. I've gotten a little bit off track from what I came here to say. A lot of what I just typed didn't make it into the homework writing, the professor said keep it brief, which this isn't. The main point I tried to make in the homework was that we all exist in our own realities. Perception is powerful. You are what I think you are, because in my world you don't exist outside of my mind, just as I don't exist outside of yours. I exist within my own mind in the truest form, but it is completely different from the form I occupy in the mind of anyone else. Everyone has unique perception which details their world based on what they attend to.

This is what I came to discuss. I introduced my friend Bugsy a few days ago. He and I have been shooting e-mails back and forth recently, sharing some ideas. He sent me an article tonight that addresses some ideas I have for a career (http://hubpages.com/hub/How-Dr-Hew-Len-healed-a-ward-of-mentally-ill-criminals-with-Hooponopono this is the link he sent me). This next bit is quoted from the article by Rosario Montenegro:

It might sound crazy or just plain metaphorical, that the world is your creation. But if you look carefully, you will realize that whatever you call the world and perceive as the world is your world, it is the projection of your own mind. If you go to a party you can see how in the same place, with the same light, the same people, the same food, drink, music and [atmosphere], some will enjoy themselves while others will be bored, some will be [overenthusiastic] and some depressed, some will be talkative and others will be silent. The "out there" for every one of them seems the same, but if one were to connect their brains to machines immediately it would show how different areas of the brain would come alive, how different perceptions there are from one person to the next. So even if they apparently share it, the "out there" is not the same for them, let alone their inner world, their emotions.

As I read that it sounded exactly like what I think about the topic of perception so I wanted to post it here. The article is very interesting and I recommend reading the whole piece. I think there is truth in many varying forms in the world. I find truth in this article. I'll need to study it more in depth. Bugsy has tried sharing it with me in the past, but I guess I wasn't ready to think about it then. My interests have changed or my capacity for understanding has grown or something. The ideas in the article are something I am interested in learning more about and folding into my personal philosophy. I am becoming more and more "anti-label" when dealing with people, so in this frame of mind I find some of the labels applied in the course of the article to be unnecessary, but I'm not one to get politically correct. The topic of the article isn't degraded by the label of "crazy." Just don't forget that there isn't any "us and them," we are all the same human species. That's my opinion.

The Declaration of Independence

People, denied their right to liberty, banded together and declared independence from the greatest empire in the world. It wasn't a declaration based on selfishness or desire for power. They weren't thinking *'it's my way or the highway'* in regards to British rule. They were not being defiant to the king like a teenager is to their parent. The founders of the United States were motivated by humanity. They were not perfect, nor was their revolutionary approach perfect. They were doing something that none of them had ever done before. They were framing a new government and country.

We can sit back in the comfort of our private homes 234 years later and say what they did wrong through our 2010 lens, but if we do, we do so without justice. We do not know the full context of the era in which they lived. What we do know is what they wrote, but even then it isn't a perfectly accurate picture of life in those times. It is impossible for us to divorce ourselves from our current standards and norms. We can see that they were not power seekers. They wrote the declaration out of **"decent respect to the opinions of mankind,"** not exactly the language I would expect from war-loving conquerors. The Declaration of Independence was an expression of grief by an abused population which inadvertently set forth a model for what human rights are. By defining what specific treatments from a governing body are unacceptable, the Declaration established what a list of rights ought to consist of.

To anyone who thinks this document no longer applies to governance in our day I say we need this document now as much as ever. The same goes for the Constitution, which is obviously written in attempt to right the injustices outlined in the Declaration. Personal liberty and responsibility were the desired goals of the founders, not total control and absolute power, which seems to be the case in (all of) our government today. The final sentence from the Declaration: **"And for the support of this Declaration, with a firm reliance on the protection of Divine Providence, we mutually pledge to each other our Lives, our Fortunes, and our sacred Honor."**

This pledge ought to be hoisted on banners throughout our country and across the earth. Whether directed to King George or to tyranny in general the Declaration is a standard for **"unalienable rights"** for all. It is time for another American Revolution. The enemy is not a tyrannical government, though some might argue it is. The enemy is not amassed in uniforms on a battle field, though that type of enemy is available if we seek it. This time the enemy is each citizen of this country, ourselves included. We who have become complacent with the liberties and freedom we have been divinely blessed with, we are our own enemies. We are constantly presented with choices. Some might think they can choose not to choose, but this is not the case. When the choice is liberty or captivity, there is no neutral ground. Either you choose liberty or you don't. I want to choose liberty.

Progress on the Whimsical Revolution Thus Far

Yesterday morning I read my first couple of posts on this blog. In the very first one I explained that my revolution wasn't on the macro level, but rather it was a personal revolution. I think great change on the macro level has to begin with individual people changing and then harmonizing with others around them. It is like changing and tuning strings on a guitar. You can't magically change them all and have them in tune in an instant. Each string needs to be detuned to release the tension, and then removed. Each new string needs to be strung up and then tensioned individually, but in conjunction with the other strings. If you tune your E to E and then begin to tune each other string successively you will find that the tension on the E has changed by the time you finish the sixth string. Fine tuning a guitar requires multiple passes through the set of strings, fine tuning each as you go. After several courses the strings will be in their proper tune and will be unified with the other strings in the proper key.

I think people are similar. When you want a revolution, for good or for bad, each person involved needs to change independently of others, but still in accordance with others. You can't expect them all to turn out the same, some will be tuned to E, others to D or A, but together they will be in unity of purpose. This is why my revolution is one of self. I can't do anything to effect a large scale change of thinking in society, but I can do something to effect a large scale change of thinking in myself. This is what I thought about as I reread that first posting. I didn't think about it much throughout the day, but in the evening I became very introspective. [As an aside, to finish the guitar-revolution analogy, when new strings are put on a guitar and tuned up, they don't hold that tuning for very long.

There is flexibility in the strings and they will stretch. Retuning is constantly necessary for the first few hours or days the guitar is played, depending on how much it is played. Eventually, the strings will be adjusted appropriately and they will maintain the tuning. In applying this to people, I would suggest that new ideas and change in people need to be reinforced for a while until the person is sufficiently able to maintain the change of habits and ways of thinking.]

I will need to set the table for this next story; otherwise you might be trying to eat your spaghetti out of a mug. You could if you want to, actually, maybe you should. I'll still give some background information. January of 2008 brought me to this university. My brother had been attending here for about two years before I got here. He had his group of friends, not unlike the cast of a sit-com. They developed their own sovereign nation, New Massachusetts, NewMa for short. Within NewMa there were all of the necessary political leaders. While the country maintained independence, they were still loyal to the United States and lived peaceably within it. The boundaries of their country consisted of whichever apartment the majority of them were living in. The motto was "Brotherhood Until Marriagehood." This was strictly adhered to. I would have had inclusion in this society due to my blood lineage with one of the founding fathers of it, but by the time I arrived at school most of the NewMa'ns were already moved on to marriagehood or graduationhood. Those who remained were working intently on obtaining marriagehood as well. The pie parties, *Charlie Brown Christmas* parties and whatever other formal events of the past were no more, or more accurately, not as frequent. I was able to participate in a few events. It was just that one semester though, and then NewMa was pretty much finished.

The remaining remnants were a rug and a door magnet that read "NewMa main office." I must address the door magnet first. I call it a door magnet because it was on our front door; I suppose it could be any sort of magnet though. Our door was already special in that it must have been replaced some semesters back due to damage, because it was different than the other doors. Highlighting the difference was the fact that our door didn't have the apartment number painted on it. We had a different style door without a number, and it had a magnet that said main office on it. This was entertaining to me when confused college students would knock on the door and then see that it was a regular apartment and ask with perplexed look and tone, "is this the office?" I'd say "yes", then pause, and then say "but not for the apartment complex." I enjoyed it. The other remaining relic was a rug. It belonged to a member of the country who had graduated two semesters prior to my attendance and was off at grad school, I think. He is a professor here now, so he must have gotten an advanced degree. Anyway, I never met him until last night.

This rug was a bit of a celebrity in NewMa. It was similar in appearance to a *Twister* mat, only not as brightly colored, not plastic, and not with circles. The rug was all squares, different colored without pattern. Dark colors, such as maroon, and dark blue, and some muted beige type thing. At one point in the NewMa history the rug did serve as a *Twister* mat; a unique spinning pointer wheel thing was made for the occasion. One time my brother was rolled up in the rug and carried around, finally to be unrolled from the rug from above the sofa, making him roll down to the floor a la a Bugs Bunny cartoon. I wasn't present for these events, I only saw pictures, but it was enough to make me feel at home when I moved into the apartment and the rug was present. I have been in school for 7 semesters now, and that rug has always been in the living room. The whole time I was told that the owner would someday return for the rug.

Through my first 4 semesters there remained a founding member of NewMa in the apartment, but after that the duty of rug guardian fell to me alone. My new roommates didn't know the story of NewMa and didn't quite understand the door magnet. Last fall the doors were repainted and the magnet came down. I mailed that to my brother. The rug remained. I started mentioning it to the members of NewMa who I retained contact with, that I would soon be leaving and that rug would be on its own. Last week, James Johnson, of jamesjohnsonfineart.com called me to inquire about the rug.

It was a Friday night, I think. I was home, sweating in the heat, watching TV. James called and the first thing he said was "I'm at [some water/amusement park]." I told him my situation and thanked him for calling to let me know that. I thought that was all he was calling for, but then he got down to business and told me that the owner of the rug would be coming for it within the week. Last night he arrived. He has been teaching at the university for a while, so he's been in town and wanted to recover the rug, but he didn't know where it was. He asked James, who then called me and the rest is history. It was nice to finally meet the friend of my brother other mutual friends, we had an enjoyable chat and laughed for a while. We joked about how I was told that one day someone would show up asking for the rug. It was very Biff and Marty-*Back to the Future II*-sports almanac-like. Only no one pulled a gun or threw a matchbook holder at anyone's head. It felt mythical though. And when he had left with the rug I felt like something had been accomplished, or rather not accomplished.

This is when the introspection began (that was some back-story!). I spent the next 4 hours after that thinking again about my revolution of self and just the last two and a half years in general. I asked myself questions like these: am I any better off now than I was before I came to school? In the last few months have I progressed or am I complacently stagnant? If I get hungry for pizza over the weekend, should I walk somewhere or pay the delivery fee? Eventually I was able to fall asleep, but the pensiveness remained when I awoke this morning.

It is interesting to see what events will trigger the thoughts or actions that lead to change; a simple joke between two weird guys who never met before, about the mythical guardianship of a rug. This sends me into a spat of introspection. I suppose it is actually quite proper, after all, it is a *whimsical* revolution I am trying to lead.

August is Already Over

That was fast...August, I mean. Feels like it was just July.

I've been watching the major cable news stations and the response to Glenn Beck's Restoring Honor rally from this past Saturday. I've watched the rally and listened to the messages delivered. I am pretty sure that none of the commentators speaking about it have. If they did watch, they didn't understand it, or they are making up what they wanted the rally to be. They are reporting their agenda (or I'm simply interjecting my agenda now, touché). I call that propaganda. I wonder what the animosity is based on, the animosity against Beck. If he is as the commentators call him then why such the big deal about him? They try to paint him as inconsequential and full of hot air, but then why do they keep talking about him? Is it simply because they think it is easy to make fun of him? I suggest that they keep talking about him and slandering him because he is speaking the truth.

At least what I believe to be the truth, and I recognize that. Not everyone sees the same things as being truth. That's fine. If we don't agree, great. Let's discuss it and be friends and see how we can teach each other, because I think most people have something good to share with others, regardless of political or religious or social points of view. So why can't Keith Olberman allow that Glenn Beck believes differently and appreciate that? And the same goes for Beck. I think the aggressive attacks on Beck are because some people can't accept the fact that others believe differently than they do, and they feel that they need to make everyone believe as they do. That is dangerous. If you don't think the same way I do then you probably think what I'm saying is hypocritical, and perhaps it is, or at least sounds that way. I know I have a hard time hearing some things and accepting that someone believes that without trying to run it through my perception of truth. But I try to.

I guess I just have a hard time understanding how someone is going to attack Beck for encouraging faith in God, hope and charity. Have faith, be responsible for your self and your family and your neighbors. Alveda King, at the Restoring Honor rally, talked about how we need to see past skin color and realize that we are all a human family. What's wrong with that? Nothing. Why are we a human family? Because we are all children of God. We are all a family because God created us and we are his children. But I suppose that's just what I believe. It happens to be what Glenn Beck believes and a lot of other Americans as well. So what about that makes us racists or hate mongers? That's something I've been thinking about.

You know what else frustrates me? People who want to be victims. Sociology calls them conflict theorists, well, not really, I guess what sociology calls a conflict theorist, I call a person who wants to be a victim. Perhaps it'd be better to say that conflict theorists study those who want to be victims, oh well. Conflict theory is one of the main theories of sociology. Marx would be considered a conflict theorist. This theory says that all problems are caused by people with power. Whether it is men having power over women, white people in America having power over black people in America, or rich people having power over poor people, it is all a big power struggle. Everything is conflict. I think that when conflict becomes your reason for everything and your lens through which you view the world then you are embracing contention and anger.

I joke about being an angry guy, and sometimes I get more frustrated with certain things than I should, but I think for the most part anger isn't one of my key characteristics. And I hope to root out that weakness entirely. It isn't a happy way to be, always finding fault in people and placing blame. Playing the victim. That's what anger and contention do. It comes down to selfish pride. You feel like you deserve something and if you don't get it then it must be because someone else is preventing you from getting it. You play the victim and if there isn't a real oppressor, because sometimes there will be (i.e. Hitler), you have to have a make believe oppressor. May I suggest a rich, white man? This type is the popular target from many conflict theorists.

It bothers me when people don't accept responsibility for getting the things they want or need. If you are capable of getting it, then do it. If you expect someone to hand it to you without work, then I'm saddened by you. An interesting note from Beck's rally, afterwards the area of the rally was clean and free from litter. After the last presidential inauguration the area was trashed. Perhaps Beck paid people to pick up the trash so he could use this comparison as a feather in his own cap, or perhaps the people who attended his rally are responsible people who work for what they have and take care of themselves while the people attending the inauguration are expecting a handout from the government because they are "entitled." Something to think about. Or I'm still being what I was condemning earlier.

I'm not perfect or close to it in anyway. When I look at things that I don't agree with and try to theorize solutions I'm not trying to single anyone out, I'm making generalizations. And I include myself in the audience. I don't think you have to be perfectly honest to recognize the importance of honesty and the wrongness of lying. If you had to be perfectly clean to understand what clean was then no one would ever understand what clean is. Does that make sense?

Finally, I was talking to some folks tonight and one of them said something about rhetorically asking God how long he can see the injustices of the world and stay his hand. She wasn't asking how God could let bad things happen, but rather how long will he allow us to go so wrong in so many ways. In my mind I thought a possible answer to that question might be "How long can *you* sit by and watch these things happen?" I believe that we are agents to act for ourselves. With this being the case, we have to be free to succeed and free to fail (did you hear that Government? Free to fail). When we see injustice across the globe and wonder how *God* can let it continue, perhaps we should wonder how *we* can let it happen. Perhaps we ought to see how we can fix it. Maybe that's what life is about. God knows how to fix these problems and he has always told us the solutions through prophets. The resources are there, we just need to care and seek them out. Do we have faith that God is there and that he has given us the resources? Do we have hope that we can achieve these good things? Do we have charity, or love for others, enough to fight injustice by carrying out what God has taught us? When I contemplate these questions I feel a bit of guilt. This is what the revolution is all about. I've got to change. I need to revolve. This isn't the first time I've had moments like this. They always seem to hit, last for a bit and then fade into the distracting sources of entertainment that are so plenteous these days. Change is possible for everyone with the mental capacity and function to do so, which means most of us. If you desire to change then you can do it. The difficulty comes in maintaining the change; preservation of self-improvement. That is the topic I need to give some time to.

House or Howser?

I made a comment to Muffin Man yesterday about *Doogie Howser* and *House*. I'd like to delve further into thought about the two TV doctors. I'm wondering which would be a better guy to have checking you out when you are ill. House is obnoxious and self-centered, but he has been around for a while and he knows his diagnostics. Doogie is elementary school compared to House, but he has more of that "bed-side manner" about him. House would probably make fun of you and burn your face with his cynicism, and then leave you to an intern or custodian to treat your burns. He is heartless and uncaring. Probably because of his constant prescription pain-killer induced high. There's one reason to prefer Doogie, he's not drugged up and he keeps meticulous records of his life on his personal computer. I wonder if he ever upgraded from the DOS prompt. That's neither here nor there. Whatever that means. I like to type phrases that people always say, and then say "whatever that means" afterwards. We always say those things but who knows what they mean anymore. And *that*, is neither here nor there, let's move on.

When you get right down to it, when you cut to the heart (doctor topic pun) of the matter (patient), I think you've gotta go with House on the strange diseases and Howser with the common malady. Here's why: House is a master diagnostician, he'll figure out what the weird symptoms you are expressing mean. He'll insult you and make you feel like trash, but you'll already be so stressed out because of the unknown ailment that it won't really matter. The "Doog" wouldn't know where to start with your problem. He'd be your friend and solve your relationship problems, but while you are enjoying your complimentary lollipop in the waiting room your knee cap is going to explode and you'll die. He's just too inexperienced for the difficult cases. Looking at the common stuff, its Doogie Howser hands down. It's something treatable, you know what's wrong before you get to the doctor, and you just need some advice, pain killers or anti-biotics (does that need to be hyphenated?). Doogie will help you out quickly while displaying his kind demeanor. In this situation House would ridicule you six ways from Sunday (can I hear you say "whatever that means?"). You wouldn't be all that stressed out about your sickness or whatever, but House's commentary on your appearance or something would increase your stress level, thereby reducing your immune system further. Each doctor has his strong points and weak points. I wouldn't completely write off either one.

Tools and Opportunity

Recently I heard someone on the news say if people have tools and opportunity they will make things happen. I'd like to think that is true, but I'm afraid that it probably isn't. Not in every case. I do think there is still a majority of people who are willing to work, and that's good. I also think that there are a lot who aren't willing to work and while these do not make up a majority, there are too many in this group. I'm usually preachy about not creating "us and them" labels, but there are some obvious classifications among people, and this is one of them: willingness to work, or not. Maybe I'm hypocritical on this point. Maybe it is just as wrong to group people into "criminals" and "law-abiders" or "mental ill" and "normal" as it is to label people as willing to work or not willing to work. Maybe there can't possibly be a no-labels society. Even if this is the case we can still control how we view and treat groups which we label as "them." But that's another story.

My question is about just how much people are limited by environment and how much they are limited by desire. The context in which I heard the comment about giving people the tools and opportunity and letting them make things happen was in a community with the classification of being the most obese in the country. Overall, the people in this community were collectively larger than the residents of any other community. A woman in the community challenged her neighbors to lose weight and began workshops and exercise programs community-wide to help them. She said that once they were given access to the resources necessary the people were able to make the appropriate changes to remedy their collective health problems. It was a good example of how people who were limited by environment were able to make things happen. I don't want to take away from their success, but I begin to wonder why they weren't able to make changes personally. Why did it take a community organizer to inspire them? Did they really not have access to nutritional information and the ability to walk before the organizer came along?

I agree with the statement that people are limited by resources, in some cases, but I think that there is a greater problem of limitation by desire. I congratulate the people who got out and exercised and improved their health. But I don't think it was lack of resources that limited them. I think it was a lack of desire, which was probably a lack of hope. I would suggest that the woman who organized the activities and education introduced hope, not resources. It is hope of achievement that overcomes limitations of desire, which is what I would target as the real culprit. I think we are limited more by our desire than by anything else. When a person has desire they are able to overcome other limitations, like the lack of resources.

Maybe not the most smile-inducing example, but look at the ingenuity of inmates in prisons as far as the ideas and tools they manufacture. They are extremely limited in resources, but they can still create weapons and tools to escape prison. Their desire makes up for their limited resources. Again, I know that isn't the happiest example, but it makes the point. We can focus on our lack of resources and opportunities and not get anything done. We can stand outside the burning building and lament "If only we had a hose to connect to this hydrant!" Or, we can do something. Anything. It will always depend on the situation, but if you want to effect a change you usually can to some degree. Hope creates desire and desire can (though not always) overcome limitations on resources, tools and opportunity. We need to take responsibility for our individual selves and "think outside the box." Find new and better ways to do things. Don't wait for someone else to cure the disease or come up with a better process, do it yourself. And then share it.

Knowledge and Wisdom, All Summed up in a Blog

My friend Christal (www.christalcollette.com) invited me to discuss the difference between wisdom and knowledge. I quickly thought of this statement: **Knowledge is knowing what to say, wisdom is knowing when it is appropriate to say it**. I think that sounds pretty impressive; if I were to follow my own sage-ness, I'd stop typing right now. It looks like I am still working on that wisdom portion. I just want to explain that this quote sounds so good to me that I am debating whether or not I could have phrased it on my own. A quick Internet search reveals that the idea has been expressed in various forms many times before. Oh well. You can still quote me on this incarnation if you'd like. I typed it into the search bar and nothing came up verbatim. So now I call it as my own verbatim. That's right. Since I'm rambling, I will expound upon my quote. No, I will give an example. Those are fun.

Imagine Captain America. He is about to thwart an evil dictator from some foreign country, and when I say thwart, I mean thwart! I don't know what that means. Wait! I need to reset my scenario. This is what you get when you type at your thinking speed. OK. We'll keep Captain America and the dictator as our protagonist and antagonist, respectively, but we'll turn the tables on the good Captain. In the James Bond-cliche-style, the evil dictator has Captain America strapped to a table which is about to be blasted with a laser and dumped into a volcano. As the hero struggles to free himself, he tells the dictator that he will never get away with his ultimate plan. Captain America coaxes the dictator to reveal his smarmy plan to enslave the human race. If the dictator is wise, he will not say what he knows about his plan. He has knowledge about what he plans to do: the how, where and when of it all. For his best interest, however, this is an inappropriate time to reveal that information. Wisdom would be recognizing this timing and refraining from giving up the battle plan. Luckily, Captain America is up against an evil dictator who, like the Bond-style villains, is pretty capable in getting almost to the end of an elaborate scheme, but falls apart at the end. One would think that if the wisdom is lacking in the end it would have been lacking all along the way, not the case though. I'm not here to argue the logic of spy movie writers. I'm here to give a real-life application of the difference between knowledge and wisdom. And I've done a mighty fine job I might add.

In case you were wondering, Captain America makes a last minute speech about the undying liberty in the heart of every man, woman, and child in the world and how no evil dictator can put that in chains. Though their bodies may be restricted, their hearts and minds are free. One day they would rise up and overturn the evil dictator's regime. As the dictator finds himself listening intently and shaking a bit in his evil dictator boots, one of his associates, a comely lass, mixed up in the dictator's propaganda thinking she was doing something good for people, is inspired by the speech and sneaks up behind the dictator to give him a knock to the back of the head with a heavy book (camera zooms in and pauses on the title of the book: *Concussions and Why You Don't Want Them).* She quickly releases Captain America who does whatever it is he needs to do to stop the evil plan and get his rescuer away from the volcano. In the final scene of the movie you see the lass and the Captain parting ways at a bus stop. She's off to college to pursue micro-financing He gets her e-mail address and promises to add her on *Facebook*, but you know he won't, he's Captain America! He's too busy for *Facebook* and comely lasses.

So there you have it. Wisdom and knowledge. Knowledge is the process and wisdom is the application. I hope that clears things up...if you were befuddled. If you were clear, I hope you are now befuddled.

I Am What I Am, But is That Really What I Am?

Some things just are. These are what we call facts, or truth, but is there a difference between fact and truth? I think there is. A fact is something that is proven and observable. It is a fact that water is wet. Obviously, that is also truth. Water is wet. In some cases what is fact is also truth. On the other side there are facts that are not founded in truth. Fact is here and now, what you see is what you get. Truth is eternal and independent of people, time and place. Fact depends on those three things. Not all fact though, it is a confusing comparison to make between fact and truth. I guess what I'm driving at is that just because some idea or belief is accepted as fact because a majority, or even a loud minority, says it is so, doesn't mean that it is true. Facts that are true have to be independent of the taint of man. Anything coming from God is true. I don't think man can create truth, only manipulate it, for good and bad. When things that aren't true are called fact and attempts are made to pass it off as truth then you have bad manipulation of truth. Good manipulation of truth is found in some science and medical understanding. Manipulation is one of those words that have a bad sounding reputation, but it is a fine word, it means to work with or control. What it boils down to is that you have to be careful not to be too quick to accept fact as truth and to thoughtfully consider the source of all information you receive. I think we all have access to the source of all truth for confirmation of truth. Maybe the fact vs. truth question is unimportant, but seeking to know and understand what is really true is well worth our while.

If You Don't Pay Now, You'll Pay Later

I don't know if it is society-born or what, but I've noticed that getting something for nothing is bad. I've mentioned this in other posts before. The thought keeps coming up in conversations and when I'm watching the news and stuff. After breezing through college like I did, and seeing so many others do the same, I began to apply this thought to myself. I'm not saying I cheated or was dishonest in my schooling, but I didn't put much effort into it. What did I get? A 3.67 GPA. That's what it's all about anyway, right? Just get the grade and diploma? Well, I think that is the mindset of a lot of people these days. Just get the results. If you can do it without putting in the expected amount of work, then you are all the better, right? I don't know.

I just bought a truck last week. I put more than half of the price down and then financed the rest. I didn't have the required amount necessary at the start, so I got some of this truck for nothing. The result is that I now have to pay more than the original cost in the form of interest on the loan. By not paying now I am paying later. I think usually the paying later is going to be worse than the paying now. For my education, I probably shortchanged myself in some ways by not putting in the effort to really learn and internalize some of the concepts. I think it would be interesting to have a standardized test given to entering college freshman, one specific to their major, and then give the same standardized test to graduating seniors and compare the two grades. My guess is that the scores would be slightly higher on the way out, but not by much.

Maybe I'm too critical on myself though. Perhaps school was easy for me because the school I went to was easy (which it was), or because I'm super intelligent (well, you know). Still, I know I could have put more effort into studying. Someday perhaps I'll pay for it. Then again, I know where to look for certain bits of information, so unless I'm on a game show and have only 30 seconds to come up with the answer I think I'll be OK. Maybe that destroys my claim that not working hard in college is getting something for nothing? No, it doesn't. It is logical to see how minimal effort in school results in getting something for nothing.

I'm not going to be like everyone else and say that things are always better appreciated if you work for them yourself, but sometimes that is the case. I've had things given to me that I appreciated quite a bit. I hear people say that kind of thing often. I think parents on TV always say it to their kids. I can imagine Danny Tanner saying it to DJ, "You'll appreciate that sweater more if you save the money to buy it yourself." I disagree with Danny, and not just on this imagined dialogue, but that's another story. I don't think it is a matter of what you get out of the thing you get without work, but that pattern of thinking leads along the lines of what I see as the underlying issue.

Getting something for nothing leads to an expectancy and dependence upon the source from where your gift came from, if it happens consistently. Obviously I'm not trying to destroy the concept of gift giving. Gift giving is good, for both parties, which is why I disagree with the thought that you'll appreciate more what you work for yourself. It isn't about that. It is about what happens to your expectations if you don't work for it. Does a person receiving welfare benefits not appreciate what they are receiving? I think they appreciate it. Would they appreciate it more if they worked for it? Perhaps, but I think what they'd really be feeling good about is having done the work, not receiving the benefit. Work contains a benefit in itself.

For example, I am digging a trench in the yard. We have a natural runoff spot along the driveway. Over the years it has taken a gradual slope-to-level surface into a bit of a canyon. There is a snaking track along the driveway that is only a few inches wide, but the overall valley that has been created is too uneven to drive the lawn mower across. I've devised a plan to allow for drainage while leveling out the ground so that it can be mowed. If I was to wake up tomorrow and it was done I don't think I'd be less appreciative of the functionality of it. I would enjoy the fact that the hard work was done and I wasn't the one to do it (although I do enjoy doing the work, so I might be sad about that, but there are plenty of other projects to work on, so it would be okay overall). I don't know where I'm going with this now. I guess it shows that gifts are good. It also shows that you (or at least I, maybe I'm alone in this) don't appreciate things less if they are given to me.

Finally, the point I was probably trying to make is this: when you get something for nothing, you miss out on the benefit of the work itself. I would miss out on the new knowledge and experience that would be acquired through the task. I would miss out on the physical exercise the work would require. I would miss out on the creative exercise of my mind that would be needed for the project. All of these things serve as satisfaction in a job well-done.

When I worked for the State of Vermont as an imaging specialist (scanning documents and indexing them electronically) I never felt like my job was very demanding or important, not the paper aspect of it. As my friend Harris (the one that discussed the pay and performance rates of pro-athletes with me) said, my old scanning job was so easy even a monkey could do it. I didn't argue with him. Well, I did, because monkeys can't do the keyboard number pad as well as I can, but superficially looking at the job a reasonable person might think a monkey could do it. I'm getting distracted again. I felt like the job was pretty basic, but I was still satisfied when I accomplished a lot of scanning and indexing. There was something satisfying about that huge pile of papers being processed. Empty baskets were pleasing. Had someone else done the work I don't think I would have been offended, unless it left me without the ability to get paid, then maybe. But that wouldn't have been about my having done the work or not.

What I'm saying is that while the task itself was nothing ground-breaking or world-saving, the process of doing it was still satisfying. I didn't appreciate an empty in-basket more because I emptied it, but because I became something new through the process of emptying it. Even when the task is as seemingly insignificant as scanning a stack of papers there is still learning and experience that occurs. By not working now we miss out on having that knowledge and experience later.

That's my message. I enjoy typing up these posts because usually I just take an idea and start typing, not doing drafts or revisions, just letting my thoughts flow and typing it all up. (I type down. Why do they say type it up? Perhaps because the paper scrolled upward on a type writer? The text moves in an upward direction on the screen as I type, but the keys are down and my fingers press down on them to type.) So do I appreciate my blog posts more because I put in the time to type them or do I get more out of them because I'm the one putting in the effort? Probably both in this case actually. The moral of the story is to not tell people that they will appreciate the end result more if they work for it themselves. Tell them that they will gain more out of the obtaining phase if they do the work than they ever will in just the receiving phase. That is, by working to earn the money to save to buy the sweater they will gain much more than they will in the receiving portion, which is the simple satisfaction of having the sweater they wanted. In either case they can obtain the sweater (whether by work or gift) and in each case they can appreciate the sweater, but they only become something better as a person if they worked for it (unless it is a *really* cool sweater).

Yay! Sleep! That's Where I'm a Viking!

I just discovered that I spend roughly 38% of my time sleeping. It doesn't seem possible. Or does it? I kept track of my activities last week for a project. It only covered 5 days, however, so it wasn't a full week. I don't know if it can be called an accurate sample of my time spending behavior, but I will treat it as such nonetheless. When you break it down to hours in a day and the recommended amount of sleep, I'm not too far off the mark. 24 hours in a day divided by 8 hours of recommended sleep (I read it somewhere) equals 33% of the day being spent asleep. Roughly speaking. You get the idea. So while it was initially shocking to think that I spend that much time asleep, factoring in the recommended 33% makes my 38% seem not as lazy and idle. So I sleep a little more than 8 hours a night. Does that really make me lazy? No.

What makes me lazy is that I spend roughly 20% of my day consuming some form or another of media; whether television, movies, music or the Internet (such as *Facebook*), right there I'm spending half of my day either asleep or lying around watching TV or watching my *Facebook* newsfeed. Again, not *all* bad. I know how many chicken zombies my friends have on their farms, as well as whats happening in the world. I do watch the news often. These stats are all just rough estimates based on one 5 day period of time when I kept track of my activities. It is hardly a scientific study; which worries me all the more that it is incredibly accurate in portraying the type of person I really am! The aspect of this project that saves me from throwing the television out the window is that I spend equally as much time, percentage-wise, working as I do consuming media. Being unemployed, financially, at the moment, my working consists of yard stuff. I was surprised to see that I spend a nearly equal amount of time working as I do being entertained by various media, surprised, but pleased, or at least mildly content.

The disappointing part of this whole project is that the work I am doing is largely for my own satisfaction. I like the exercise and spending time outside, which means that by adding together my media consumption time and my working time I'm spending 40% of my day seeking to please my own interests. Tack on 38% of the day for sleep and I spend 78% of the day following after my own desire. I am a hedonist, at least for 18 hours a day. But that rings true with my thinking that we are all hedonists. I don't think we can clearly label ourselves as strictly meeting one man's philosophy or another's, but I think there is a lot of truth behind the hedonistic approach to human motivation.

Hedonism is portrayed as sensual and dirty in a lot of cases, but it isn't. If you have ever slept in rather than get up early to help someone out you were acting hedonistically. It is putting you above others and doing things to increase reward and limit pain or punishment. The controversial part of hedonism is when you try to see how it jives with religion. Unfortunately, I think a lot of religious activity is hedonistic in nature, but that might not necessarily be bad. It's a tough call. One recurring theme in religion is to please God. I have no complaints with this. He is pleased when we serve other people. So if we are serving other people to obtain a pat on the back from God, then we are serving other people in order to serve ourselves. Hedonism. Also, there is the desire to avoid eternal punishment that motivates people to serve. Hedonism again. Along these lines is where I think hedonism finds merit. But where it seems to fall short, at least in my understanding is that it never allows for a person to transcend this base level of motivation. Hedonism doesn't allow that a person might actually divorce themselves from any expected return and serve in a truly self-*less* manner. I believe it is possible to be selfless. I think we are able to get over ourselves completely, even if it is only in one instance or one type of behavior.

I think overcoming hedonistic, or perhaps biological, motivation is what charity is. Charity is the love of Christ, the love of God for his children. It is the motivating factor that makes life possible for us on the Earth. Charity is the motivation and the end goal for true Christians. To obtain true charity is to be like Jesus Christ. Though no one will accomplish this in mortality, because of our natural, biological imperfections and weakness, charity is still accomplishable in fragments and portions. Perhaps if I want to reduce my hedonist pursuits from 78% of the day to something a little less embarrassing I can focus on my motivations. Why do I spend so much time seeking entertainment? Motivation is an interesting subject. One that I will not discuss any further at the moment because mine has just run out in regards to typing. I will now eat some pie.

Why me?

I just learned that if I type a title and hit 'enter' then the blog is posted.

“Why me?” is something I was thinking about earlier. We probably all ask it at some time, whether to parents or a boss, or God. There are two ways to ask it: simple and selfish. If a boss asks me to do a task, I might ask "why me?" thinking that I am not qualified or whatever for the task, this is asking it simply. If I ask in a whiney way then I am being selfish. It is either because I think I am above the task or I'm lazy, in a bad way (yes, there is good laziness, listen to "Lazy Day Afternoon" by *The Plain White T's*, well, maybe there is no good laziness, but it's a good song). So we can ask "why me?" in different ways. Obviously we don't want to ask it with a sense of pride. That's all. My thoughts ran out on this one. I need to get a voice recorder and carry it around. Sometimes I'll think of a topic and start writing it in my mind. By the time I get to the computer I've lost some or all of it. Such is the case this time. Let's see if I can salvage the topic.

I suppose the point I wanted to make was that often when we have an experience and we ask why, it is because we are shortsighted or selfish. We either don't understand how the experience will work for our good, or we don't want to get our hands dirty. I have no closing thoughts or moral to sum up. I guess one last thought is that if we find ourselves asking "why me?" to someone we trust, maybe we should just trust them and follow their recommendations. And for those of you who might be a bit more on the pessimistic side, there are of course people who will be asking you to do something out of their own selfishness, in which case you might ask "why me?" Can't really do anything about that, I suppose. I've got nothing on this thinking thing tonight.

Crime Doesn't Pay

As I was driving yesterday morning I saw a man leave a bank and enter the road, on foot. He stopped between some parked cars and waited for an opportunity to cross the road. He was probably expecting me and other drivers to stop and let him cross. Just as the Santa Barbara Police Department has a saying (probably on a T-shirt) "No body, no crime," I have a saying "No crosswalk, no stop." Cold and heartless? Of course not, jaywalking is a crime.

Though not even a misdemeanor in some jurisdictions, it is usually at least an infraction. The typical punishment in either case is a minimal fine. Money isn't the issue though, it is safety. I confess I am an occasional offender in this case. I do jaywalk at times, but I feel I do so responsibly. That is not to excuse myself, as I would never excuse a criminal who was responsible in robbing a bank or committing a murder. "I plead not guilty to robbing the bank. Sure, I held a gun to the man's head and pushed him to the ground, but the safety was on! Obviously I took money that didn't belong to me, but I said please!" That might have the markings of responsibility (it doesn't), but it isn't responsible. I jaywalk when the road is clear and I do not pose an interruption to the flow of traffic, that's my goal for being responsible about it.

The way I see it is that I am capable of crossing a road without dying, so I will. If that means not using a crosswalk, then sometimes that's the way it is. Any person who steps in front of a moving vehicle and expects that vehicle to stop is a jay, a rube, an imbecile. In the battle between moving vehicle and me, I don't stand a chance. I'm not going to chance it, hence my claim of responsible jaywalking. Of course, wherever jaywalking is a crime, I do not endorse the practice of it, responsible or otherwise. I suppose the only real responsible street crossing is to obey traffic markings and signals and employ active observation of traffic. I never walk anywhere any more so I don't have much need to cross roads. But that's mostly irrelevant.

I decided to read some facts about jaywalking so I typed it into the search bar on the browser. I checked out the *Wikipedia* post for it (http://en.wikipedia.org/wiki/Jaywalking) even though school taught me that you have to be careful with that site. I think it is informative for basic things like this, but I wouldn't cite it as a reference, well, you know, in a real piece of writing. This blog is "casual Friday" about that kind of stuff. Yes, I did just use that phrase in that context, feel free to do so yourself. Example: I am casual Friday when it comes to matters of foreign policy. Back to the Internet search; I found this section of results interesting:

First result: Ticket Trouble…New York Post

Second result: Pedestrian hit by car survives…Whittier Daily News

Third result: Chinese not warming up to clothes dryers…Austin American-Statesman

Cue singing: "One of these things is not like the others." What do Chinese folks and dryers have to do with jaywalking? That's what I want to know. If you find out anything, let me know. I suppose I could have clicked on the link and maybe found out, too late now.

Back to my original thought; as I was driving and saw the man who obviously wanted to cross the road but was not at a designated pedestrian crossing area I wondered if it is possible to be an accessory to jaywalking. Many crimes have accessory charges associated with them. Perhaps there can't be an accessory to an infraction though. I guess in most cases it just hasn't been legislated. It probably never will be as the general rule is that pedestrians in the street are given the right of way, common sense dictating. That's not to say it is fair game to run over people not in a crosswalk, nor is it to say that if you hit someone who irresponsibly jumps out in front of your car that you are fully responsible. Maybe you are, I don't know. The point is, if I had stopped to let that man cross the street when he wasn't on a crosswalk (he was pretty close to equal distance between two crosswalks) then I would have been an accessory to his crime. I don't need that.

I think it would be entertaining to see someone get charged (as long as that someone isn't me) with accessory to jaywalking. I'd also like to see someone picked up for conspiracy to commit jaywalking. If someone walking along the road starts walking towards the curb, maybe takes one step into the road and then steps back up and keeps walking on the sidewalk. It could be argued that they were thinking about jaywalking. I guess these issues aren't really that high on the priority list. But wouldn't it be sweet if they were? How about if the worst crime being committed was jaywalking? It'd be a nice place to live. Or we would adapt our ways of thinking so that jaywalking would be as morally reprehensible as murder. It would take some time, but it would happen. I guess. So be careful out there.

What? No references to Jay Leno's Jaywalking bit? There's one

No Animals Were Harmed in the Typing of This Blog

Have you ever seen at the end of a movie that some animals *were* harmed during the filming of a movie? I was just wondering. They always have that note declaring safety to all animals in order to appease the animal society people, but I wonder if they can make that claim honestly. There are a lot of movies with animals in them. I know people sometimes get hurt during the filming of a movie (I wonder why there is never any notes about *that* at the end of a movie, is human safety not worth as much as animals? Probably has something to do with informed consent, I'll allow that).

Animals must get hurt in the filming of these movies and then they still make that claim. Who is checking up on these people? Is it possible that during the filming of *Free Willy* there was a catastrophic accident and the whale died and then they found a new whale and passed it off as the same one? I wouldn't know. A lot of animals look the same (within their species I mean). I wouldn't know if they started with one dog and then finished with another one. No one would know. It's almost like the movie people are trying to exercise *Jedi* mind influence on us. The sad thing is that it is working. Or maybe people just don't care. It makes you think a bit. But that's all. I will guarantee that I have never knowingly hurt any animals while typing my blog. More importantly, I have never hurt any people with the typing of my blog. Unless I have offended someone's feelings or ideals, and that is possible. But then that part of the injury isn't covered by the animal claim, so it shouldn't be covered in my people claim.

The typing I am doing is the counterpart to the filming of the movie. The movie people stop after the filming is done. Their liability is over. If an animal is harmed in the watching of their movie they aren't responsible; they don't *claim* responsibility anyway. Perhaps that is when the responsibility is even more important, or is it? Then we are approaching the violence of video games influencing the behavior of children. Where does my responsibility end with this blog? If I say something inflammatory and then someone punches someone, am I liable? This is probably why the movie people leave the disclaimer at animals; it gets too complicated when you add in people with their agentic (think free will) living style. That's not to excuse people who create materials for the purpose of causing uproar. They have their freedom to do so, but they have to accept the consequences. Anyway, I was just wondering if you ever saw a note that said animals were harmed during the filming of a movie, advertently (my own word) or inadvertently. As you were.

Help! You Need Somebody!

I like to point out things that I think are in error. Be it a person's idea or action. Humans are very discerning creatures, though creatures is used here in a literary sense, to introduce neat sounding words, I think the word subjugates our animal distinction and takes away our unique divinity. Now some of you might take issue with the fact that I am associating humans with deity, more on that later. I say we are discerning, and I mean that we constantly have to discern, or to decide, between different options. We are always making choices. We are free to choose, but the options are dependent upon the previous choices we have made.

I studied psychology in college. It was my choice. This course of study prepared me for certain options in the future. If I now decide that I want to be a doctor of medicine, I have not previously made the choices which will allow me to make this choice without further choices and passing time. My choice to study psychology limited the options that would be available to me in certain areas in the future. In some ways we determine our futures by our agency. The future is not determined for us but by our own choices…for the most part. I do believe that there is divine providence which interacts with the course of our lives for good, but this influence is probably going to be dependent upon previous choices we have made, though I don't intend to command what God can or cannot do, I believe he can intervene in our lives without our preparing the way, but I also believe he greatly respects the gift of being agents unto ourselves which he gave to us.

I believe that liberty to choose is one of the natural rights, or inalienable rights, which was pertinent in the founding of the United States of America. There are also some limitations to our total liberty based on the liberty of others around us. Sometimes the choices of others can heavily influence our total liberty in options and choices. Cue our more recent, say, 90 years worth, government of the U.S. In some ways they have impeded our liberty through selfish legislation. Which brings me back to my original thought: I like to point out when I see someone or something which I think is in error. The question that springs from this thought is this, who decides what is right and wrong? Further, when is it appropriate for me, or is it, to instruct someone else about their error and suggest correction?

I do this all the time, if not out loud then in my head. I hear a comment from someone and think about how much I disagree with it and imagine a correction to the comment. I wonder if it is my place to say anything though, so usually I keep quiet; depending of course on the situation and my relationship with the person who I am judging to be in error. I expect that you might feel unsettled by the suggestion that there is any one person who can determine who is in error and in need of correction. That uneasiness about this topic is what generated my question in the first place. Personally, I believe that Jesus Christ is the judge of all people. So where does that leave me? Do I just keep my mouth shut and let whatever happens happen? No, of course not! If that were the case we wouldn't have any laws. We have laws because while living on this planet we must govern ourselves. We have been taught the laws through prophets and by Christ himself. For those who accept Christianity and the accompanying commandments, there is recognition of the law and the Judge. But not all people do accept this belief system, so there are man-made laws and judges (yes, judges are man-made; storks bringing babies is a myth).

We have laws and judges in place and we have law enforcement agencies and officers, but there are still opportunities, some less extreme, to see and judge and correct in day-to-day life. These are the situations I'm talking about. The best I can do is to judge acts and ideas against my autobiography. I can look through my lens and see discrepancies. Is it right for me to think that my lens is better than the lens of anyone else? The easy answer is no. But the simple answer is no, also, just a different kind of no, or perhaps neither of these answers make sense. The real answer (for me) is that Jesus taught that with whatever judgment we judge with, meaning, whatever our system of discerning and calling someone out, will be what is used to judge us. If our judgments of others are unfair, we will think our personal judgment for eternity unfair. If we judge with mercy and according to eternal laws with which we are familiar, then this is how our judgment will be. In the end, it is not discerning and making a judgment call that is prohibited, rather, it is self-righteous discerning and making a judgment call that is. We must judge righteously, that is, we must follow the laws when making judgment. The laws I speak of are the laws of God, which not everyone adheres to and accepts the same version of these laws. And this leads us back to the same question, is it OK for me to offer correction to someone who believes differently than I do?

I think the answer is to only judge and to only offer correction out of love for the person you are referring to. If your motive isn't genuine concern for the welfare of that person, then you are operating on anything but love. Love does not vaunt itself, love lifts those around it. I think a primary motivation for wanting to correct others is competition. I know this is the case from personal experience at times. I want to correct people because I want to show off my knowledge or understanding or I want to be seen as more competent and capable. These feelings come from competition.

The world speaks of healthy competition, but I'm beginning to wonder these days if there is such a thing. I blame our language, having only one word to describe competition. Maybe there is good competition and bad competition. It is similar to the issue of the word pride. Pride is bad, according to religious definition, yet people are proud of their accomplishments and take pride in their country and family. There are two meanings to this word, each with drastic difference. For my own understanding, I separate pride into these categories: self-aggrandizement and joy of accomplishment. One is bad, it puts self above all others; the other is good, it shows value in following a job through to the end. With competition there might be two categories as well, possibly the same. Bad competition could be defined as that which is for the purpose of lifting yourself above others, while good competition could be that which encourages personal growth by all parties involved. However you slice it, competition and pride have dark sides that are not fueled by love.

Contention is the root of pride and competition, I suggest. Contention is the feeling of animosity towards an individual or group. It is being at odds with another party. Contention is argumentative. Contention is "I am right; you are wrong." Competition and pride fueled by contention are the dark sides. Competition and pride fueled by love are the light sides, or Jedi sides for those of you who might prefer. Since we are on the subject, Anakin Skywalker wanted to help people, just like Yoda, but when it came down to it, Anakin wanted to help people to serve his own selfish desires. I'm not going to say that *Star Wars* is a perfect example of how one should or shouldn't align their motivations, but if we look loosely at the story as a generalization I think it works. The Jedi were selfless in the use of their abilities, Anakin was portrayed to be the opposite. Motivated by selflessness, or love, the Jedi were on the good side of the Force. Anakin, motivated by selfishness, was on the dark side of the force. To get back to my topic of thought, motivation determines when to correct another, and who ought to do the correcting.

As I try to keep the revolution oriented towards myself - I don't want to be a pompous commentator - I am keeping this topic centered on me. I want to know when it is appropriate, or if it is at all, for me to judge others and then offer correction. I feel it is almost prideful to expect that I can give correction, but then I have to be introspective and realize that I have been blessed with attributes and experience which does allow me to offer helpful ideas and suggestions to other people. Again, it can become a fine line to traverse, just like the Jedi. The lesson I will take away from thinking through this topic is to seriously analyze my motivation when I want to call someone out on something. Some questions I might ask myself are these: what are they doing that I find displeasing? Why do I find it displeasing? What purpose would it serve to voice my displeasure with their actions? How might they feel after I do, if I do? How might I feel after I do? Am I willing to suffer through the pain of change and correction if I decide to voice my displeasure? That last question might be the most important one in determining when we offer correction to someone. Am I willing to be by their side as they make the effort to change their life, if that is the choice they make and they have a desire for me to help?

This is an idea I've gotten from my brother when we have discussed these things. If we are not willing to help a person change (again, the idea that we know better than someone else is a tough one, but if we are seeking to align ourselves with the will of God, and desire to help others do the same, then in my subjective point of view, it can be done out of love and not selfish pride) then we ought not to suggest they are in need of a change. If I am not willing to put on the apron and get behind the minimum wage counter at a sandwich shop then I better not tell the trained sandwich maker how to do their job. Unless the motto of that sandwich place is "Have it your way," in which case you should probably just be polite in asking to have it your way. In any case, we should probably all be polite. Hopefully I'll keep thinking about these things and allow it to lead to improvements in my character. I will, however, retain the right to criticize politicians because I am willing to take their place, as untrained as I am, because I don't think a dog, a pony and a spider could do any worse than those self-gratifiers we have elected into office right now, and for the last several decades, generally speaking. I love to contradict myself as a grand finale. We all have room to grow.

And Another Thing

Have you ever noticed how close these two statements sound, "coming!" and "come in!"? These are two things that people yell when there is a knock on the door. Two very different messages being delivered, but two very similar sounding phrases. If I yell "come in!" and the person hears "coming!" then the person will stand outside the door waiting and I will sit in my chair waiting. Eventually the person knocks again and I yell again and then it just gets uncomfortable and socially awkward. But, if I yell "coming!" and they hear "come in!" it is *so* much worse. Have you ever had that one happen? You are in your apartment and the knock at the door and you yell "coming!" and then the door opens and some boppo's head is poking in your door. I don't know what a boppo is, but I don't want him coming in my house when I'm not prepared for him. My advice is to always keep your door locked and not to yell commands to people who knock. Seriously, why would you yell for someone to let themselves into your house when you don't know who is out there? So keep the door locked and approach visitors with caution. But you don't have to take my word for it. It's your life, do what you want with it. Just like J.G. Wentworth suggests you do with your money. And Goodnight!

Well, There's Your Problem

From capitalism to communism, liberalism to conservatism, there are plenty of -isms to blame for all of life's woes. Here's one you are probably familiar with, but don't know it yet: mine-ism. It isn't a political ideology, but people are loyal to it. It isn't a theological ideology, but people reverence it. Mineism takes the worst bits of all of the other -isms and rolls them up into one nasty bit of personality deficiency.

Capitalism lends the desire to succeed and accomplish and gain more. Capitalism provides the freedom for people (who put forth the required effort) to succeed. When it gets out of hand, capitalism can become a hot-bed for greed. Greed is the downside and greed is what capitalism shares with mineism. What can I get? That is the mineist's question. Actually it's more like "What can I get?" and "Give it to me now." I think give it to me now is the motto of the mineist.

Communism lends the need to pull other people down. In communism, it isn't enough for you to work hard; you need to make sure that everyone around you is working just as hard. There are no rewards for those who are willing to put in extra effort, only punishment because their work isn't rewarded. Mineism has the attitude that no one else is as good as you so they don't deserve what they have, and instead you deserve it because you are you. After all, who could be better than you? Self is supreme. So take that piece of communism that says no one deserves more than you and add it to that "Give it to me now" mentality.

Liberalism lends entitlement. You have a right to housing, food, education, nutrition, automobile safety, a job, etc, etc, etc. You are entitled to everything, says liberalism. You needn't work for it or put forth any effort. This is the bad side of it. It is good to support other people and for all of us to take care of one another, but it is not right when it comes as a mandate from the state. Social programs and entitlement programs are essentially state mandated care for others. It takes the ownness off of the individual and puts it on the collective. When you take responsibility away from the individual you hurt their ability to be self-reliant; you destroy their ability to be independent. Mineism thrives on entitlement.

Conservatism is harder to pinpoint the bad side because it is where my bias lies. To me conservatism is what society now calls "traditional values." To me it is faith in God and the right to life, liberty and the pursuit of happiness (also the originally planned word "possessions"). Of course there are no perfect -ism generalizations, so I'm not saying that all non-conservatives are god-less and don't support the basic inalienable rights factored into the founding of the United States of America. I am saying that this is the way I view conservatism and as it is the politically related label that I would apply to myself, if I were to apply any, so I am less likely to look for and notice the bad aspects of it. But they are there. I guess it isn't harder to find, I'm just less likely to see it right away. Enough of that, here's the mineism-conservatism connection: close mindedness.

Conservatism gets a reputation of close mindedness partly because some people labeled this way are very dedicated to their beliefs which they have put a lot of work and thought into developing, and the other part is because some people are just close minded. Again, I don't think being close minded is a monopoly held by conservatism, but I do think that it is the biggest downside of the -ism. Mineism is completely close minded.

Mineists don't care what you think or what might be better. To a mineist, if they think it or they want to do it, it is the best way. Take your empirical research, science and testimony based on personal experience and throw it out to sea. The mineist knows whats best (for everyone). Mineism is the worst -ism of all.

We are all mineists to some degree. "Mine" is a dangerous word, with and without the word "land" attached to the front of it. With it, well, you get the idea, but without it it can be just as explosive and fatal. Other than our ability to be agents for ourselves in making moment-by-moment choices, what can we really say is our own? What really is mine other than agency? Even the power of agency has been given to me by God, so while I exercise it, it wouldn't be mine without His gifting it to me, so is it fully mine? I guess it is, but the resultant consequences aren't fully mine, if I accept Jesus Christ and allow his atonement to cover me.

To me, the sum of all of this is that we have to do as John F. Kennedy suggested and ask what we can do for our country. But not just our country, also our family, our friends and everyone else we see. It is good to work hard and acquire items that make life livable and comfortable. It is good to seek to improve the lives of all people around us. It is good to be understanding of people and their individual situations. It is *not* good to seek gain for pride, or to push people down to make ourselves feel higher, or to ignore the needs of others in pursuit of our own interests, or to take away someone's independence and give them everything for nothing.

I don't fully know what mineism is. I had the idea tonight and I've tried to brainstorm a definition in the typing of this post. There is something plaguing society today, and at the very rootiest rooty root (I can't type seriously for very long without having to throw in some bit of nonsense) of it is pride. Pride is the easy culprit, to which humility is the easy antidote. Though not easy in doing, only easy in defining. It seems too broad to be able to generate a solution for it, but since pride is the root, and pride is an individual issue, maybe it is the best target to aim for. What do you think?

The Last of the Red Leaf-hicans

Fall is having a midlife crisis. About a month into it and just less than two months until it is officially over. I just took a picture of a few lonely red leaves hanging from an otherwise bare tree branch. The red leaves are the last ones in the area. Then I noticed a tree across the creek that is full of bright yellow leaves. I captured the image with the red leaves in the foreground, the gray-blue water of the creek in the middle and the bright yellow tree in the distance. I think it turned out to be a pretty solid picture. Red, yellow and blue; primary colors, right? Dig it.

Now for something entirely different. A few days ago I was chatting with Bugsy. We got on the topic of movie content ratings and decency standards on television. I guess that's what we were talking about. We talked about how smoking used to be cool in movies and on TV, and now they are thinking about making smoking a reason for a restricted (R) rating for movies. If you have too much smoking in your movie it will be rated R. Then Bugsy suggested that they'll have to start blurring cigarettes when they play those movies on TV. I think that is a funny concept, but with these nut jobs out there it seems plausible. Think about it. Every year the content on TV seems to be getting "edgier" and more risqué than the year before. People are wearing less and less clothing and using more and more abrasive language. So I see this change coming to movies on TV. The blurred spots will leave naked bodies and occur over a lit cigarette. Then rather than bleeping swears they'll start bleeping the word cigarette. I guess it depends on what you see as the more dangerous image, people smoking or people naked. I have a solution.

My solution is this: specialized television channels. When you order cable or satellite you pick out specific channels you want. No more of these package deals with 6 versions of the *Home Shopping Network* and 4 different *CSPAN*s. In this way, you can control what types of shows are being brought into your home without impeding the entertainment desires of other people. I think the best case scenario would be that the worst stuff on TV just wasn't being made, but realistically, I don't see that happening. Rather than censorship, just change the way the product is obtained. *ESPN* is strictly sports and *CNN* is strictly news; *CSPAN* is strictly boring and *MTV* is strictly idiotic. They can then make channels that are strictly high decency standards and ones that are low decency standards. You might be thinking, "well, don't they already have that?" Have you watched the channels that are supposed to be targeted towards children and families? The *ABC Family* channel plays a lot of stuff I wouldn't watch with my family.

Maybe this solution is terrible. The home shopping channels probably think it is. Who would ever request those channels specifically? Three people. That's probably it. I suppose that is why they get grouped into the package deals. Well, tough luck. Why should people have to pay for 70 channels when they only watch 6 of them? So 5 dozen or so channels go off the air? No one else has jobs these days, so they can just join the crowd. I don't mean that, I'm just typing things. Correction, I was just typing things.

Where is the Line Between Flattering Imitation and Legal Plagiarism?

Some movies are remade after a few decades to bring a story to a new generation. Some of these movies are successful. Others ought never to have been made. One of these remakes was the 1997 made-for-TV version of the 1957 classic *12 Angry Men*. I have not seen the remake, so I guess I can't slam it too much (not that lack of knowledge has ever stopped me from expressing opinion before), but I am a fan of the original film version. The original movie was nearly perfect, so I don't see any reason for it to have been remade. It seems to me that it is just an attempt at profiting from old success. *12 Angry Men* tells a timeless story of integrity and humanity. How can you improve on perfection?

Well, I can't think of any other movie remakes that weren't necessary except for *Miracle on 34th Street*, *Annie* and *Charlie and the Chocolate Factory* (you know what I'm talking about, I don't remember the exact names of the Gene Wilder and Johnny Depp versions). Each of these movies was sufficient in their original state. This is a pretty subjective topic though. And a case could be made that the newer *Chocolate Factory* with Depp as Wonka is more accurately based on the book, which I haven't read, but I'm going to stick with my preference for the Wilder version. Anyhow, flattering imitation or legal plagiarism?

This process also shows up in television when a popular series is turned into a movie. This line of thinking has nothing to do with my original intent behind this posting; I'm just using it as to segue into mentioning something. I thought *McHale's Navy* was a remake of a movie, but it is a movie version of an old TV show. So I had to change the subject slightly so I could say that anything with Tom Arnold is unnecessary. That being said, we return to the intended topic.

I am a romantic. Whatever that means (according to the second definition of the word romantic at dictionary.reference.com it is to be fanciful and impractical). I like the movie *You've Got Mail.* I think it is a nice story. I don't know how relatable it is to me; I'm not a rich bookstore owner like Tom Hanks' character, nor am I an out of work former little bookstore owner woman like Meg Ryan's character. Regardless of being able to directly relate to the characters, I like the story. I only learned recently that it is a remake of the movie *The Shop Around the Corner.* If you are familiar with *Got Mail* you will know that Ryan's store is called The Shop Around the Corner. Now that name makes sense. I finally watched the original movie last night. I like it.

Jimmy Stewart played Tom Hanks (use your imagination, you'll follow what I'm saying) and Margaret Sullavan played Meg Ryan in the 1940 film. The story had some subtle differences. Strike that. The two stories had some subtle similarities, but most of the details were entirely different. Could you watch one and then the other and not realize they were the same story? Of course not, but you can watch one and then the other and not feel like you just watched the same movie twice. Both are good, but *The Shop Around the Corner* is probably a little better.

I would say that in the battle of Hanks/Ryan vs. Stewart/Sullavan, the verdict is flattering imitation. Whereas with *12 Angry Men*, the verdict is legal plagiarism. Since this is my blog, I am not going to give evidence for either declaration.

Unemployed is a State of Mind

Last week I decided to make an official declaration in the revolution: I am no longer unemployed. I don't have a job, exactly, but I am not unemployed. I am constantly employed by various activities. Unemployment in the job market is a problem, as it means people aren't able to financially support their families, but no one should ever be wholly unemployed. There is always work to do. Being unemployed is a choice that needs to be made by the person being unemployed. I've been unemployed financially for a few months, and I've decided that I'm not going to be anymore. If that doesn't make any sense, don't worry, this won't either.

In order to reconcile my unemployment, I've decided to call myself a writer. If people ask what I do for work, I will reply that I am a writer. Technically speaking, I am a writer, but so are you, anyone who knows how to draw symbols for the purpose of communication is a writer. Purposefully speaking I am also a writer, because I write things, like this blog. Financially speaking is the way of speaking which I need to incorporate into my being a writer.

I am trying to get the financial aspect incorporated through a web page called Helium.com. I've spent a week participating in the Helium community and I have earned 19 cents. Not a living, by far, but it is a start. The program works with your participation in two tasks: writing articles and rating articles. It is a community operated business, a co-op. All of the people associated with Helium write articles, on thousands of titles across hundreds of topics. Some of the writers are professionals, some are enthusiasts, and I imagine many are like me, nobodies. I don't have any specialty, I am not an expert on anything, yet I am writing articles that are used to answer people's questions when they do a web-search. I suppose. I think that's how it works. All I know is that I can write articles about anything I can think of, and if those articles are good enough, I get a few pennies for them every month representing revenue sharing with the web site. For me, it is an enjoyable hobby. I don't expect to be able to earn a living with Helium, but getting paid to write is one of the career choices I had around the age of 12, and to see it come to completion now, even for a simple 19 pennies, is fulfilling.

Come On, Shoes!

I have spent the majority of the last 8 hours sitting at this table. I'd say dining room table, but I don't know that this area of the house where we have the table we dine on can really be classified as a room. It's more of a "way" than a "room." Perhaps a "space." I've been sitting at the dining space table all day. What have I been doing? Retying my shoes. Seriously, I've retied each shoe twice while sitting here. I can't even begin to understand how a shoe unties itself while on a foot that is just hanging around under a table while the owner of that foot types on a computer. If it was one retie I wouldn't give it any thought. Even if it was two reties on one shoe I might just dismiss it as an anomaly specific to the shoe, but two reties on each shoe? That's unreal. Especially since I always double-knot my shoes and I never have to retie my shoes while I'm out and about. But, an epiphany, the running around that would logically seem more likely to disengage a shoelace knot probably enacts forces on the laces which secure the knot, rather than loosen it. Those forces are not being applied in the same way as my feet rest restlessly under the table. Or maybe the dog keeps sneaking over and untying my sneakers.

One other thing, last night I was thinking about how people always complain about being at the end of their rope. I don't know why they complain, I was at the end of my rope and I found a kickin' tire swing.

Quote of the Day

The whole point of getting things done is knowing what to leave undone.
- Oswald Chambers

I don't get it. That might come as a surprise to some of you, but I don't get a lot of abstract quotes. I don't know what makes a saying quotable. I assume it has to do with universal generalizability of the wisdom being shared, but then quotes like this one sneak by. The "point of getting things done," meaning, the end result of doing things, "is knowing what to leave undone." Why would I do things just for the sake of knowing what not to do? It plain doesn't make sense. I do things to get them done, not to know what not to do. I didn't go to school to learn what I didn't learn, I went to learn what I did learn. What do you think this quote means? Let me know. I'm lost on it.

Watch Out for Cats

A few weeks back my friend Bugsy was telling me about a pond nearby that is man-made and stocked with some fish. Apparently, putting fish in a water-filled hole in your backyard attracts heron. The heron that have come scoping out this new fish pond are from the other side of the tracks, or clouds, whatever the bad type of birds are on the other side of. These birds murder fish. The pond owners started finding their fish dead, stabbed right through. I'm not sure if they saw the birds doing it or not, but that's the story being relayed (I apologize for not checking my facts on this story, but given the possible danger, I think it best that I keep myself under the radar. You might wonder if it is good for me to be blogging about it then, but don't worry, birds don't read blogs). So the fish are dead. The birds are killing the fish and not eating them. This means that birds are murderers.

At this point in the story that Bugsy was giving me, I wondered out loud, "I thought humans were the only animals that murdered." We laughed and that was that. But then it wasn't that. It became a serious discussion about murderous animals. It seems on first consideration that animals typically only kill when they need to defend themselves or their young, or when they want to eat something. Humans kill for those reasons, but some, possibly defective ones, kill for other reasons, such as anger or injured pride. Based on the brain structure of animals, when compared to humans, it doesn't seem like they have injured pride, or even pride at all (have you ever seen them eat? or not wear clothes? no pride). So animals should only kill for "legitimate" reasons, right? Why are these birds killing fish then? It makes no sense. Especially since I've never seen heron around here before, they must be taking a long flight to get here, and then they just kill the fish and leave them lying around. Horrible. Anyway, we tried to come up with other animals that killed for more than just food or defense. Cats.

Cats will kill squirrels, birds, rodents, anything small and weak, like themselves. Then they will take the corpses and put them on your doorstep, kitchen table, or bed. They almost seem like they are showing off. You might think, that's pride, cats kill out of pride, but I suggest that they don't kill out of pride, they kill for the pride. Cats have instincts to kill and eat. Domestication hasn't taken that out of them completely yet. The killing drive remains intact in cats. Here's the catch, they don't need to kill because they are fed by their loving owners. Why kill and eat a nasty mouse when you have gnarly smelling cardboard cold cereal stuff? Exactly. Cats are well fed, but they feel the need to kill, so they do. They are programmed to kill and bring food back to their pride, their family, so that's why they put the dead mouse on your bed. You are their family. Cats and humans are the only animals that kill for the thrill, but really only humans, because cats are just doing what genetics tells them to do. That should suffice.

Given this overwhelming collection of facts (not facts) lets return to the fish-stabbing heron. If they don't have pride issues like humans, they must be being fed somewhere else, and therefore are not hungry, but feel the need to kill, like cats. It's gotta be one or the other, right? The real question now is this, where are the heron being fed? This is the investigation that I need to do. If I don't return, avenge my death.

Check Your Science at the Door

The creator of the phrase "Sticks and stones may break my bones, but names will never hurt me!" needs to check their science.

Honestly, can't names do real damage? I think so. It is unethical, but you could try it out for yourself. Just find someone you interact with regularly and start calling them jerk all the time. It won't take long before you see the effect. I strongly recommend you take my word for it. Don't try this at home, it is dangerous. This is why I suggest the following alternative to the school-yard saying.

"Sticks and stones may break my bones, but names may upset the chemical balances in my brain, thereby altering my emotions, cognition, and behavior." – Ajax

I'd go on about Becker's Labeling Theory, but I just don't have the writing spirit right now. Just know that deviance results from a label. A name. If you are called something you become that something. Meaning that names are powerful and can hurt you. It also suggests that names can uplift a person. And if we are going in that direction then we also have to allow that sticks and stones can not only break bones, but build houses. Sticks could also be used to splint the very bones they have broken. This is getting out of control.

I will recap: Sticks and stones may break your bones, but sticks might help them heal later, and furthermore, sticks and/or stones might be used to build a shelter in order to protect further damage from being done to your bones. Names will never hurt you, if they are kind and supportive names, which inspire a person to become something new and better.

Names will hurt you if they are given in a mean-spirit. People react to how they are treated, unconsciously, so they don't even have to decide to be hurt by names for those names to hurt them.

Well, it's not perfect, but I could revise it some time and then all of the kids could start reciting it on the playground. Actually, I think it is well-meaning, if ill-informed, parents who keep the "sticks and stones" saying alive. Those parents ought to read this post and change the world. I'll go eat something now. Cheers!

Science: The Great "Distractor"

I have nothing against science so far as it is the empirical gathering of evidence in attempts to better understand the world around us. I do take issue with science becoming a *distractor* from living life. I feel like there is a tendency for some people to focus so much on what science says that they miss the purpose for life. They spend their lives worrying about asteroids they see on telescopes millions of miles from the earth, or melting ice. These things may be real dangers, but is there really anything we can do about them?

In regards to global climate change, I personally don't believe that people are big enough to destroy the planet. It might be possible, but I don't believe it. I think that God created this planet for a specific purpose, which is to give his children (all people) experience, and that purpose won't be defeated by people (not on a full scale). Part of our experience is to learn and make decisions and act as agents according to our own will. It is this freedom to act that makes me leery of saying it is impossible for us to destroy the earth. I don't think it will ever happen, but if we have complete freedom to act then we must have some ability to do it. I do think there is a degree of arrogance in thinking that we are going to destroy the planet because of our actions. Either arrogance or contempt.

However, we are responsible for the earth. If we act recklessly and waste things ungratefully then we will destroy ourselves, but not in the way of climate control. We are stewards of the planet. Animals included. Other people included. We need to look at why we are alive and how we fit in with the environment, animals and other people. We do have the power to destroy, but we also have the power to build and encourage.

Don't be distracted by the *stuff*. I know I need to make some changes. There is a lot of focus on 2012 and whether or not ancient prophecies about the end of the world are accurate. I don't know. It might be. I'm not going to focus on it, but I think that perhaps 2012 can have an amazing impact on the lives of everyone on the planet, if we choose it to. Rather than focus on the doomsday theories, we can all look at our lives and make the necessary adjustments. 2012 could be life changing for the global population. Hopefully it will be for the better. It starts with each of us individually.

Packaged Deals

Sometimes you just have to take the bad along with the good. This is evident in variety bags of candy. Recently I purchased a hefty amount of discounted Halloween candy. It is great to have a good sized box of candy on hand. As I eat away at the candy, I notice that there seems to be less and less of the Snickers and Life Saver Gummies, and more and more of the Milk Duds and Jolly Ranchers. I don't know if the Duds and Ranchers were represented more proportionately than the other candies were, but I know they are now. The Duds are good, but too chewy. The Ranchers are tasty, but too hard. As I look at the candy box now I wonder if these two types were thrown into the variety bags to get them to sell. I didn't purchase either of them intentionally; they were just part of a collection of something else that I wanted.

Do candy companies make candy that no one wants? Is it possible that these less desirable types were thrown into bags with more desirable types just to get them out of the warehouse? Could there be a more egocentric approach to candy distribution? The answer to all three questions is no. The point is that this is what I thought of when I was looking at the box of candy with all of the little yellow boxes and thin plastic wrappers. For no other reason than that I simply don't like them as much, I thought the Milk Duds and Jolly Ranchers were disliked by everyone. Does this have any relevance? Of course not, candy is candy. Discrimination regarding candy is perfectly alright.

If I used my *candy frame of mind* as my *people frame of mind* then you can see where problems might arise. And if you can see it, then share it with me, because as I think back over this example I'm trying to figure out what I mean. I don't mean that if I see a large population of people I think that they are disliked and the manufacturer is simply trying to move his product. I don't mean that at all, but that's what I seemed to be implying by my statement of comparison. Originally I was only going to comment on how I thought that less favored candy was paired with more favored candy to get rid of it. But then my interest in society crept in and I started making connections. It just so happens that in this case the connection failed. Now, on with the show.

Packaged deals can either be a win/win for the customer or a win/win for the manufacturer. In either case, when it is win/win for one it is probably a win/lose for the other. For instance, Conan O'Brien is doing a contest of some sort. I saw a commercial for it (see www.teamcoco.com for more information). In this contest he is giving away 20 pine tree shaped car air fresheners. But that's not all! He is also coupling a new car with the scented dangly tree. It's a packaged deal. Win/win for the winner, as they get two good products. Win/lose for the sponsor as they give out a cheap thing and an expensive thing. In sales, only slightly different than with giveaways, a packaged deal usually tries to couple a great thing to a not-so-great thing in order to make the not-so-great thing sell, or couple two not-so-great things together to make them seem less not-so-great.

If movies featuring The Rock aren't selling, perhaps you couple them with movies featuring John Cena. Zing! I don't actually have much experience to make such an accusation, but I know they are both TV wrestlers, so probably good targets. I actually like John Cena, from what I've seen of his non-wrestling work. I haven't seen his wrestling work outside of the incessant commercials. Cena was on an episode of *Psych* and he was entertaining. Also, I've seen The Rock in some movie or another, and he's an actor, as good as can be for also being a TV wrestler. I'm having trouble recalling his name. I could just look it up, but I choose not to. Again, I'm getting way off track, the point of this (poor) example is that when you have one mediocre movie, it might not sell well, but if you couple it with another mediocre movie and call it a deal then you'll have a better chance of moving both. Win/win for the seller and win/lose for the consumer. You might think it would be lose/lose for the consumer, but they are getting two movies, usually for the price of one, so that's really not so bad, even if the movies feature TV wrestlers in the lead roles.

Now that I've alienated the TV wrestling fans, here are some other packaged deals I thought of that couple bad stuff with good stuff: winter and cold, great power and great responsibility, and eating donuts and failing health. I'd like to suggest a new combination. How about coupling eating donuts with great power? It only makes sense since great responsibility and failing health are already coupled together. Think about it. Fin.

Recipe for Humor: Literal and Out of Context

I don't think this title makes any sense. I guess you can just eat it then. I'll give you a general idea, I'd say gist, but I never know how to spell gist. Actually I spelled it gyst and then searched for it and found that that is not at all what I mean. I also searched jist, which is urban slang for just, apparently. Finally I tried gist, which is the main point, and I have subsequently replaced my initial typing of gyst with the intended gist. Feel free to eat that as well, if you would like.

Once in a while people say things that if you give proper attention to you will see that they didn't give proper attention to what they said. I give you that sentence for proof. Man, people just don't think before they speak. But that's alright. It gives me something to take out of context, or make overly literal, and then laugh at.

Tonight I heard someone say that someone took a nasty fall. Now, given the context, I know that the fall was nasty, but I wonder, aren't all falls nasty? Can you ever fall and not be injured or embarrassed? Perhaps; it depends on your emotional and physical constitution, but I know I've never fallen and then remarked on how pleasant it was. Saying it was a nasty fall isn't necessary. I'm not so sure anymore if this is an example of taking something out of context. Let's just say it is and then leave it at that.

This post seems to be falling apart as I type. I had an idea, but now as it fleshes out, maybe it wasn't exactly how I thought it was. Whatever that means. I'll just give you an example of how I think literal scrutiny can alter the message of words. The local news was reporting on a traffic accident. The anchor said "they" (whoever that is) don't think that speed or alcohol were factors in the accident. Okay, I'll allow that they can rule out alcohol so quickly, but really, you don't think speed was a factor? What happens in a traffic accident? Something hits something else. Some form of speed needs to be a factor. If neither of the colliding objects were moving, then they'd never collide. Speed, no matter how slow it can be measured, is a factor whenever two things collide (even if it is one moving thing hitting a stationary thing). It is physics, or something.

Speaking of physics. I was splitting wood with some friends a week or so ago and we got a huge, knotted-up log stuck on the wedge. In case you are not familiar with the process of splitting wood with a hydraulic splitter, I recommend watching a documentary about it. This one gnarly log was totally jammed, fused even, onto the wedge. We pushed on it, kicked it and threw other pieces of wood at it. We put another piece of wood on the slide and tried pushing it into the jammed log in an effort to force it through. No dice. No success either. You see that? I used a phrase that, taken literally, wouldn't have made any sense. Of course there weren't any dice. Maybe this post is going to turn out okay after all.

Back to the stuck piece of wood and physics. I had the brilliant idea that leverage would help put more force on the wood. I grabbed a longer and thinner branch; thinner than what we were splitting, it was probably still 4 inches thick. I used the branch as a ram and slammed it into the stuck piece of wood. One hit knocked it off. Before I had swung it, I told my comrades that physics was the answer. So when my plan was successful I threw down the branch, raised my arms triumphantly and jubilantly shouted "Physics!" I think it was the first, and it may likely be the last, time I have ever jubilantly shouted that word. I remember thinking about working that physics story into a post, but I don't think I ever did. Now that I have, I hope it was worth it. If I already have and you are aware of that, thank you for reading my blog so faithfully. Cheers.

Cruel and Unusual Punishment, Alive and Well

The 8th amendment to the U.S. Constitution prohibits cruel and unusual punishment. Sometimes the Supreme Court interprets the Constitution to figure out how it applies to life in this country. The Supreme Court has never set forth a ruling regarding solitary confinement of prisoners relative to the 8th amendment. What could we possibly do to people that is crueler than keeping them locked in an 8' by 10' room for 23 out of every 24 hours? Perhaps it is time for the high court to do something controversial that I might actually agree with. That sentence sounds very self-serving. And so it is.

I think solitary confinement is the cruelest punishment, worse than death, and it ought to be eliminated from the corrections system. It represents the selfishness behind criminal justice. Why do we have a criminal justice system? To protect the innocent, maintain order in society and rehabilitate offenders. At least that's what it's usually billed as. Unfortunately, I think the emphasis usually falls solely on the efforts of protecting society and punishing offenders. I believe in the law of consequence, so I'm not anti-punishment, but I do like the idea of not making it cruel or unusual. Of course, I don't really know what unusual means and I could do without that part of it. I think there are some unusual punishments that are not necessarily cruel and might be rather effective. I digress. I think punishment is acceptable, if it is done appropriately with the correct intention. But I don't think that punishment should be the only focus in criminal corrections. Why not help people improve their lives along the way?

Sure, it is easier said than done. You can't force someone to change their behavior. Not without seriously damaging their brains. People have to want to change. Someone with tendency towards crime has to want to stop being criminal before they can really stop the deviance. This is what makes involuntary incarceration necessary. Some people are penitent and wish to change, but are still incarcerated, involuntarily. There doesn't seem to be any way around incarceration. I think there are some crimes that shouldn't bring with them a sentence of prison, but that's for another discussion. Solitary confinement is for the purpose of punishing convicts after they are already in prison. Solitary is the prison for the prison society.

My primary concern with the prison system in general is that it tries to teach people to live in civilized society while placing them in a perverted version of society with all new folkways and mores. How do you teach someone to play basketball on a baseball diamond? I think it is difficult, at best, to rehabilitate or properly socialize a person in prison at all. Then when you take them out of all social contact and put them in a small room alone for 23 hours a day, forget about it. Everybody needs somebody. We are social by nature, when the ability to socialize is taken away, the individual suffers. I like to spend time alone, but the thought of being in a small room all day without any contact with other people makes me feel claustrophobic. I can't imagine being locked up in solitary confinement. Of course, I can't imagine being locked up in prison. On the surface it seems like I'd rather leave the general population to have some respite in solitary confinement, but that is a very superficial thought. The situation would have to be really bad for me to want to leave a community and enter into solitary confinement, even if that community is the prison population.

People act how they are treated, more than we recognize or want to accept possibly. If we treat people like they are good for nothing but to be cast off, which is exactly the message of solitary confinement, then those people might begin to act that way. Supporters of capital punishment (which I am not) and those who support the tough on crime movements probably have some questions for me. One question might be regarding how I think we ought to treat criminals. I don't think we should pat them on the back and say "you killed that guy really well, good job!" Not at all. I just think we ought to offer some options for a person to truly reform their behavior if they are willing to. You might ask "what's the point?" That is the question to answer. We all have to answer it for ourselves individually as well as collectively. What's the purpose of life? To lock up people who offend us so that they can never offend us again? Is it just so we can make our lives more comfortable? Yes, we all make our choices and reap the consequences, but what of forgiveness, mercy and compassion? Do we just write people off? Who do we write off, and when?

I watched a National Geographic documentary about solitary confinement, which is what got me thinking about this. The way our prisons are now isn’t working. It isn't the fault of the correctional officers, administrators and support staff, or really any individuals in particular. Society as a whole is the problem. We are beyond a quick fix for the correctional institutions. The underlying problem lies in the socialization of everyone in this country. It is a big problem, and it needs solving. The answers are available, but we are all too proud and selfish to put them into practice. True story. We are all in this together. How do you feel about that? Let's do something about it.

What Are You Doing Here?

Whatever happened to service with a smile? I'll tell you, it has been replaced by service with a snarl. Not in every case, but enough to notice, you will see customer service representatives showering you with contempt or retailers patting you on the back with one hand and picking your pocket with the other. The snarl can be because they hate you or because they are pretending to smile. I don't think the intent is to serve customers anymore. The purpose of business these days is to get rich and gain the advantage over everyone in sight.

But what is the world worth? Suppose you gain it all? Power, money, and fame. So what? I'm not even talking about keeping up with the Jones', we all know that that mentality is based in simple-minded selfish pride. Does that sound harsh? I hope it does, because competition over who has the most expensive or just plain "the most" stuff is childish. What my neighbor has, that I wish I had, is of no consequence to me. It serves no functionality to covet. When has coveting ever been good? No, this isn't about keeping up with the Jones', this is about a desire that comes from within the individual that just wants more stuff. I don't even know what to call it. Of course it reduces to pride, but it seems that there has to be some name for it. Selfishness doesn't seem severe enough, but I suppose it does fit the bill.

What do fame, power, and possession do for a person? These give a sense of fulfillment, but it is fleeting, much like the way drugs give a fleeting high. Like a drug induced high, the sense of fulfillment that comes from fame, power, and possession builds thresholds. Subsequent exposure requires more substance to present a similar high. This is why power corrupts. It provides feeling of accomplishment and fulfillment, but eventually you get used to it. Then you need more. Attention (fame) works the same way. Do you think it happens this way with possessions as well?

There seems to be a drive inside every person that directs their choices. The desired end result focuses the drive. There seems to be no limit to the variety of desired end results. For many the end result desired is found through religion. Others find it in basic service and humanity. Others look to a career. There are countless goals. This is where fame, power, and possession come into play. Some people place supreme importance on the gathering of these things and status markers. It is in regards to all of this that I ask the question, "What are you doing here?"

What is your purpose? If you don't know what you are doing here, then how do you decide what to do? Without a goal we are hapless creatures existing on instinct alone. We are no better than any animal on the planet. I believe we have divine nature, that we are children of God. We are on a higher plane of existence than animals because of this relationship we share with God. I wouldn't say we are better, as they too are creations of God, but there is a different relationship, which holds greater responsibility and greater privilege, held by humans.

I can only say subjectively that every person has a greater end goal than fame, power, and possession. It is an objective truth to me, but I have only subjective experience to support it. I offer that it can become an objective truth to anyone willing to ask the right questions in the right spirit to the right source. I think it is important that we ask these questions and find answers. If I don't have an end goal then what am I living and working for? There has to be some purpose. I suggest that it is a collective purpose, possibly unrecognized by some, but still worked for, that keeps anarchy at bay. It isn't political government that maintains the peace, it is a collectively shared purpose that does. Yet so many of us, some always and others occasionally, just drift through life without purpose or reason, never knowing which way to go. I'll be so bold as to say that every problem in this world is a result of this drifting. If we each had a purpose and valiantly stuck to the attainment of that purpose, and it was a good purpose, then all problems would diminish. Not disappear, but diminish. There would still be sickness and accident, death and debate, but it would all be bearable.

This is the way to fix everything. Each person honestly ponders what they are doing here. They give it time, years if necessary. They develop a purpose that is good and then they do all they can to achieve it. At the expense of fame, power, and possession. There is something that is greater than all that man has ever thought up or put together with his hands. To find that and then dedicate every resource to it is the ultimate path of life. Every person will take an individual path, but that doesn't mean that every path is unique. We will all be rewarded with what we want the most. We show what we want the most by our actions coupled with the intent behind them. It is easy to fool others; it is even easy to fool ourselves. We might profess that we want to do one thing, but then behave contrary to it, and then reason that we have to do the one as a means to the end of the other. I don't think it is that convoluted. It is simple. Determine what we want, and then do those things that lead to it. Don't go left to go right, go right to go right. This message is as much to me as it might be to anyone else. What am I doing here, and for what purpose am I doing it?

New Year's Resolutions Are a Thing of the Past

Check it: why bother making resolutions you know you won't follow through with? How about just reviewing the things you did accomplish in the previous year. I will explain further. When you decide to do something, i.e. set a goal/resolution, you feel badly if you don't succeed. How do you feel when you do accomplish something? Goodly. That's right. Rather than start your year off with a list of things that you can't possibly accomplish, only to be continuously deflated every time you think about all the things you aren't accomplishing...I'm using an ellipsis to interrupt my improperly structured sentence...make a list of all of the things you did well in the last year and celebrate your accomplishments. Instead of periodically reviewing your goals throughout the year, review your past accomplishments. You will be happy and have more motivation because you are seeing your successes rather than your failures. Your new confidence will make you do more; essentially meeting all of the goals you would have set had you set any goals.

This is all just theory, of course. I came up with it in the course of typing. It sounds pretty sound though. I expect that if you were to really follow through with this theoretical process you would have a noticeable difference in the coming year. If anyone is interested in conducting a psychological study on motivation, comment me and maybe we can hash out a plan. I don't want to do the study, but it would be an easy one for someone to do. It just takes time. Maybe it wouldn't be so easy, I don't know. Figure it out. Track some people who don't set resolutions or review accomplishments, some who do set resolutions, and some who do the past accomplishment thing. I don't know how to gauge the results though. Some type of scales, or something, about self-worth feelings.

When it comes right down to it, I don't set resolutions because I'm not big on making lists and reviewing them, so really, I'm not going to make a list of things I've done and look back on it. Even though I won't be doing it, I think it would be more beneficial to monitor accomplishments than to set unobtainable goals. That being said, if your resolutions are obtainable, good luck to you in your life. I'm trying to sync my contact list from my old cell phone with the new cell phone I just activated. It doesn't seem to be working. I guess I won't be calling anyone ever again. Peace out.

Here's Looking at it Another Way

Christmas cards are a waste of time and money. Time and money that could be better spent on sugar cookies and watching *It's a Wonderful Life*. I don't send Christmas cards, usually. I have in the past. Honestly, I have nothing against them, but for some reason when I take a satirical approach to things, people laugh, and I like to incite laughter. So if you are a fan of sending cards, I applaud your dedication to the all-but-forgotten tradition involving handwriting and postage stamps. If you are a fan of those stationery-based form letters, you are so far from the mark of Christmas cards and greetings that you aren't even part of this discussion. I actually do think those letters are bogus. It would be like me printing my blog and mailing it to everyone I've met for the last 10 years. The reason for a blog is to say the things that many of those letter writers say, without forcing it into some one's mailbox. If it is in a blog you can read it or not; a blog will never give you a paper cut.

Back to the cards. My friend Christal (ChristalCollette.com) wrote a little bit about cards on her blog. She speaks of the generic predictability of cards and her effort to overcome that this year. It made me think about cards and how I react to them. When I get a Christmas card I read the message and appreciate the feeling and effort behind it. And then I stand it up on a shelf. After a while, it has either both blown over and fallen behind something, never to be seen again, or I take it down and throw it in a drawer. That's the best case scenario for a card. I think more often than not the card finds its way into the garbage. Not even the recycling, just the garbage. I wonder if the recyclable materials have their own form of religion in which they view recycling as heaven (eventual reincarnation) garbage as hell (slow, suffering, decomposition into oblivion).

Anyhow, cards are nice, but an e-card would be more efficient in my book. I could look at it, read it, and put it on my "desktop." I could save it for a lot longer without losing it. That is, if I wanted to. Think of all of the "Forever" stamps you'd save, as well as preventing hand cramps. Just type it up and send it off. But then again, it is the thought that counts. Maybe there is more thought behind a physical card than an e-card. Maybe not.

I'm done with this thought, I'd rather think more about the recyclable item religion. It's impossible though, how would the recyclables communicate with each other. For the stuff that goes to a landfill there would be no way for them to learn about recycling. For the stuff that gets recycled, they might be able to tell of the glory of recycling, but they still wouldn't know about the landfill. The only way it could possibly work for them is if they understand human language, but that is simply preposterous.

Merry Christmas from Ajax!

I Am Really Very Tired Right Now

Inexplicably tired. At least to me. No, that doesn't make it make more sense. Whatever, I've got something else to mention.

This one is for all of the cooks and confectioners out there. I'm wondering what the difference is between 1. fudge and 2. chocolate that has been sitting out in a car on a hot day. Is there any difference? I eat chocolate and then I eat fudge and I think, 'fudge is the same as chocolate, just softer, like it has been in a hot car.' Granted there is a slight taste difference, but there is a taste difference between different brands of chocolate as well. Nestle is no good, but Hershey’s is. Then there are the obvious taste discrepancies between dark and milk chocolate. So it seems to me that fudge could just be a meltier version of chocolate and the taste difference is nothing more than brand specific recipe. Okay, so I do know that fudge is made differently than a Hershey's chocolate bar, but the idea just hit me a few days ago when I was eating fudge and I had a Homer Simpson moment: "You know, Marge, mud is nothing more than wet dirt." Only replace Marge's name with my name and mud with fudge and wet dirt with melty-soft chocolate.

Speaking of melty chocolate, have I ever told you about the time I put chocolate chips into oatmeal? I like oatmeal cookies with chocolate chips in them, so I figured I'd like oatmeal with chocolate chips in it. Up until the moment I saw the chips melting into the steaming hot bowl of goo I honestly thought that they would retain their shape. I imagined a bowl of oatmeal with raisins and chocolate chips dispersed throughout. It never occurred to me that the steaming hot oatmeal would instantly melt the morsels of chocolate. Let me tell you, the melting was pretty much instantaneous. What resulted was an ugly color of brownish gray swirls in the bowl. And as they were semi-sweet chips, the resulting mess was not a sweet treat. Thankfully there is granulated sugar to fix any and all oatmeal related problems.

The whole event was a failure, but I am now smarter than I was. When experiences expand your thought and capability can they really be considered failures? I suppose so. In this case it is still a failure, the chocolate melted.

Random Responses and The Like

One of my homeboys - you could call him a friend - runs a blog called Random Rants and the Like (Harris Lunt is my friends name). I just read his latest post, One Voice is Not Enough, and I can't make the title into a hyperlink. I'm trying to put the link to the article in there and for some reason the pop-up menu for the hyperlink function button isn't appearing. So much for a professional looking post - here is the link:

randomrantsandthelike.blogspot.com

My recommendation at this point is that you read the article and then get back here and read my commentary. That's about as egocentric-sounding a sentence as I've ever heard. Still, go read his stuff and then come back for my observations. I was going to just leave a comment on his post to answer his rhetorical questions, but figured I'd end up typing more than a comment box can hold, so this is the better route to take. Now I can post this and just copy and paste the URL into his comment box.

The swagger of his story is that one voice alone is not sufficient to make a change, so we all need to unite our voices in a chorus for good. I agree with the end result of that argument, but I think that one voice alone is sufficient. Jesus Christ was one voice, supported by Spiritual confirmation, but one voice. There have been other "one voices" throughout history. Jesus changed the world with his voice alone, but he is God, so it is different in some regards. The great "one voices" that have been mere mortals have also changed the world. But perhaps this is just another matter of semantics and definitions. Does "changing the world" mean the final action before a universal paradigm shift? Or could it be the reveille of the united chorus? If one voice unites the people for a good cause, haven't they changed the world? Hasn't that one voice been enough? It was enough to put the wheel in motion.

That was the swagger of the story, here is the thesis of his tract: art defines culture and our art is defining us as monsters. Harris cites the Saw movie saga as one example of how we might be defined by other cultures or future generations. If you think about it, it is kind of disturbing to think that perhaps all that will one day remain of our civilization is the movie Saw. It is a horrendously disturbing premise for entertainment, from what I understand. I have not seen any of the movies from that franchise. Harris' post is a call to arms for all of us to unite against filthy and degrading works that are being passed off as "art" and "entertainment." I don't know if quotation marks are appropriate in that spot. My intent is to make it clear that I don't see degrading works as works of art. If that requires quote marks, great, if not, my apologies to you, kind reader.

As long as money is being pumped into the pockets of movie producers, we'll continue to see disemboweled people on the big screen. Unfortunately, money will continue to be spent on these kinds of things because people are using extreme forms of everything in order to feel and to fill a void they have, but are unsure what to do with. That's my thought. Harris brought up some good points: a collective voice is more powerful than one voice and a culture is defined by what it produces. We can look at those ideas and see where we fit. Are we uniting with like-minded people and uniting for a good cause? Are we creating things that we want to be defined by? I'll let you answer those questions for yourself; right now I am getting back to the topic of people being drawn to extremes.

This is where I would have stopped if I put this in the comment box on Harris' blog post; as you can see, it is good that I didn't try to type it all there. But even this next bit is relevant. Why do movies like Saw and other horror/thriller types exist? Because they elicit physiological reactions in people. Even though the deranged person mutilating a body isn't real or in the same room as you, your body reacts in some ways as though they were. When you get scared your body increases production or release of certain hormones and chemicals. You feel. For some, feeling isn't a natural occurrence.

Being locked into a rigid routine from day to day, not experiencing basic human emotions other than vicariously through television or books can make for a bland existence. Some people when dealing with depression say they did something "just to feel anything." We want to feel. Sometimes it doesn't matter if the feelings are good or bad, we just want them. I think this plays into why humans do everything they do. But when you have someone with a void, and they find a quick fix (such as extreme movies), they stick with that quick fix. It becomes a drug, which is dangerous because the acting chemical portion of the drug is created in their body. Imagine how much harder it would be to kick the cocaine addiction if the cocaine were being produced by the body? This is why it is as difficult as it is, because cocaine mimics chemical processes that are natural to the body. But I'm no doctor, so this is speculation based on some recalled knowledge from psychology classes. I think it is accurate. My blog isn't accredited so it doesn't have to be accurate, I'm just trying to provide a topic of contemplation, if you so choose to be contemplative.

Anyway, this is falling apart faster than a meeting between a successful Hollywood producer and the agent for Pauly Shore. When people have a void in their life they seek to fill it. They dig and dig and dig until they get something. There are plenty of counterfeits out there, so sometimes you find something and it works, but it isn't lasting or completely fulfilling. Personally, I believe that making faith in God your top priority above all else helps to fill the void and put all other practices of fulfillment in order. When you seek God first, you can't help but seek good things after. And when we unite our voices with the voice of God, we don't have to worry about our voice not being enough. This doesn't mean that life will always be smooth or go how you'd like it to, but it does mean that you will make progress and accomplish the purpose for your life.

Now you know what I think about a few more things.

Why the World Doesn't Need Facebook

Have you seen the movie *Superman Returns* (Bryan Singer, 2006)? In this new sequel to the Superman saga we find the Man of Steel returning from a vacation, or something. While he was away, saving someone I suppose, Lois Lane (Kate Bosworth) turned against him and wrote a newspaper article entitled "Why the world doesn't need Superman (Brandon Routh)." Or something to that effect, I might not have it word for word. She won the Pulitzer for the article. I thought the Pulitzer was reserved for investigative journalism, not op eds, but what do I know, really? Nothing when it comes to journalism.

Lois wins the award for her therapeutic venting, perhaps scathing vengeance was a part of it as well, but she recants her opinion when Superman returns (hence the name of the movie, nice work keeping with the basic naming structure for Superman movies: Superman, Superman II, Superman III, etc) and saves her family from annihilation. Oh yeah, and she finds out (or did she already know?) that Superman is the father of her son. You know what that means. It means that Cyclops (James Marsden) isn't the boy's father. Amorality has infiltrated the world, sadly. Where is Superman when you really need him? Setting a bad moral example for children everywhere. If that had been the crux of Lois' argument then I'd be on board. But now I'm just being judgmental over fictitious characters. I digress.

Having given you this background information, and before I write the article "Why the world doesn't need Facebook" I want to say one more thing. If Pulitzer prizes are given to writers of opinion pieces, and my anti-Facebook thesis warrants reception of one such prize, I will gladly receive it. I am not requesting, expecting, or banking on winning the prize, or even being considered, but I will accept if it is offered. If Lois Lane gets one for an opinion, which is so ridiculously one-sided, vengeful, and wrong, then why not give one to me for an opinion that is sound and beneficial?

As I was driving home from work today I saw a teenager walking down town. He was wearing skinny jeans, and wearing them low. I didn't think it was possible for the emo-band-style skinny jeans to sag. They look so dreadfully tight, hugging out every chance of air between fabric and skin that I would never have imagined they could sag. But sag they did. Why would I relate such a story? Because it was different. It struck me as being out of place. It was new to me. I found it humorous. I wasn't laughing at the boy, just the trends and styles of his generation. Which perhaps is my generation, I don't know when a generation starts and stops in regards to trendy clothing. The kid is probably half my age, you make the generational call. Anyhow, I saw it and I wanted to share it.

I first thought about texting my friend Christal, because I thought she would get a similar sense of enjoyment out of it. Then I thought I could post it on her Facebook wall. This is when I realized that we don't need Facebook. The wall is just a text message for everyone to see. It was at this point that I asked myself why I needed everyone to see this text message. What was it about that message, and in turn all messages, that I need to have become public knowledge? I could only come up with two reasons for making private messages public: childish revenge and selfish indulgence. And then I realized that that's what blogging is for! I don't need Facebook because I have a blog! And you could have a blog, too.

Facebook is a public way to communicate with your friends, and their friends, and their friends and their friends and their friends. Eventually I guess it gets back to you and you are reading your own wall post and laughing at the poster's misfortune and then realizing it is actually your own. According to an episode of *Law and Order* that I watched yesterday, no e-mail message is safe and private, so maybe the privacy issue doesn't matter, but I still think an e-mail or text message or phone conversation is the best way to go for security and to avoid being a childish, selfish, attention-seeking wall-poster (one who posts on walls, not one who hangs on walls as a display item). But don't take me seriously, I'm just trying to make a joke and indulge in my attention seeking.

Facebook, like Superman who leaves us high and dry, is obsolete. I will not retract my statement unless Facebook comes to my rescue when a super villain has sloppily left me to die in a slow and tedious process that nearly begs for my safe escape. I don't see that ever happening, however. No, I think I will always think of Facebook as obsolete. Whether or not it was ever of great use, I don't have an opinion. I know it has been influential in the world. I'm sure it has changed the lives of many people. Well, when you get right down to it it has changed the life of everyone who has ever heard of it in some way. Once you hear of it you are different from what you were before you heard of it, when you existed without knowledge of Facebook. But that's a little more stupidly philosophical than I want to be right now. I say stupidly, but I mean uselessly. No, I don't hate on everything, although it seems to be a common occurrence with this blog lately. I guess I just have a lot of complaining to get out of my system. This is my psychotherapy.

I don't know that I have made any sound argument for why the world no longer needs Facebook, so I'll try to sum it up now. Everything that we can do with or through Facebook we can do without Facebook. If there is an alternate way to do it, then it isn't necessary. That is a rash generalization that probably doesn't hold water but I'm preventing myself from thinking about it so that I don't have to go on for another three paragraphs to explore it. I'll let you do that in the comment section below. As for me, I am finished with this post. I haven't accomplished anything with it as far as having a thesis and offering support of it. But I have typed many words, some of which might induce laughter when strung together as I have strung them together. Perhaps not. Regardless, *Superman Returns* was an okay movie. *Iron Man* (Jon Favreau, 2008) was better.

Ajax's State of the Union

I have a lot of things I've been thinking about typing for this blog. Mostly I think about these things when I am at work. I have music playing while I am thinking and working, yet I still have trouble staying awake. Someone asked me yesterday if I had trouble concentrating on what I am working on while listening to a psychology podcast (www.thepsychfiles.com). The answer is no. What I do at work is so un-stimulating to my brain that it thinks it is supposed to drop off into sleep stages. That's not official science, I'm just speculating. It sounds good in theory. I figure that when I want to sleep I try to block as much sensory stimulation as possible: no light, no sound (or a "white noise" like a fan), and blankets to cover the largest sense organ (skin). Taste and smell have never been issues for keeping me awake. I suppose smell could be in some cases, but it would be harder for taste to be the sense that keeps you awake. Again, just speculation.

Anyhow, it isn't that my work isn't stimulating enough, but it is un-stimulating. It is a negative stimulus. Five plus negative ten is negative five. This means that I have to introduce extra stimuli in order to maintain a level of arousal appropriate for staying awake. I accomplish that through music, podcasts, and mental blog writing. I feel the need to be more descriptive, as in describing the actual brain wave frequencies that I am imagining accompanying all of what I have said so far, but then I remember that sometimes I'm just too verbose, so I won't go into greater detail. If you would like to hear the descriptions, just ask the next time you see me, I'll draw it out on a napkin.

So state of the union, huh? I'll tell you the state of my union, status quo. Whatever that means. I have a job, though it is temporary and without benefits. It is simply an hourly compensation. I go and work, they pay me dollars. I'm okay with the arrangement. For the time being it will allow me to pay back my student loans. Student loans sounds like someone let me borrow some students. I'll tell you, school would've been a lot easier if I had borrowed students to do my work for me.

I'm making payments on my truck. It is a 2001 Ford Ranger XLT. I don't know what the XLT stands for; I don't think it is for "extra lettuce and tomato," as I haven't found any of either in the truck at any time. It is due for an oil change. I'll have that done sooner or later. Probably later. The truck gets poor miles per gallon, but what doesn't these days? Am I right? I guess I shouldn't complain, $3.15 to travel 12 miles is pretty good considering the alternative of walking 12 miles and taking half a day to do it, or whatever the rate of time passage would be. It used to cost human lives to walk across the country, now it just costs a few hundred dollars to drive. My life must be worth at least a few hundred dollars.

On the other hand, what good does it do me to compare my life to people who lived hundreds of years ago? We have technology now, which has changed the world so much that there really isn't any fair comparison between me driving and gold rushers walking. Or is there? People in the world today still have to walk everywhere and some might die in the process, so what was that about $3.15 per gallon? Nah, I'm not that much of a crusader, I'll still complain. But it is good to pause and think about the ramifications of what I'm complaining about. If I don't like the cost of gas, I won't drive. If I can't live without driving, well, I can, so I don't have to face that issue yet. The bigger issue to face is my own selfishness. More on that later.

I haven't played much guitar lately, or played guitar much lately, or guitar lately much, haven't written any songs. A few months ago I played some tunes with my friend Nathan and my sister Alison. We recorded drum tracks for two songs. All I needed to do was record the guitar parts and then record my sister singing and we'd have two demos. I still haven't done it. My guitars hang, un-played, unloved, un-dusted, on the walls of my room. To prove how bad the situation is, my guitar amp has become a table for the television. Perhaps it is time for that character to move out (the television).

I've been reading sporadically, but not as much as I think about how much I'd like to. I certainly am not reading news and history like I feel I should. I used to be involved and know things, but now I've slipped into a mediocre contentment. What was that topic to introspect on? Selfishness? Yes, that was it.

Summer can't come soon enough. The winter is cold and boring outside. Occasionally there is a beautiful scene involving snow laden branches or ice coatings on the trees, but most of the time it’s too cold to pay attention to those things. At least for me. I miss the greenery. I look forward to getting back outside. I have a lot of yard left to tame.

I suppose that's the state of my union, in a brief blog post way. There is more I could do to improve my station, but I don't because of selfishness. I think selfishness is the root of all problems. Call it pride if that is more familiar or comfortable for you, but selfishness hits closer to understandability for me. It is interesting that it is selfishness that holds me back from improvement. You might think that selfishness would motivate a person into doing more, and perhaps for some people that is how it works, at the expense of others, but for me I find selfishness to be occupying my time with entertainment. It is lazy and easy. Don't try to argue with me because if you look around you will see what I'm talking about.

Tonight will be the State of the Union address from the President. If you listen to the problems he mentions think about whether or not those problems could be solved by eradicating selfishness from our lives. Don't think about if something can be done, but how it can be done. Can I stop being selfish? A bogus question, of course I can. The better question is how can I stop being selfish? This leads to formulating a plan of action. Rather than addressing the problems and wondering if they can be overcome, maybe we should all start coming up with solutions. At any rate, it would make things better for me. That's a joke. I hope you get it. Good night, America.

Insert Crafty Title Here

There are two temps in the office where I work. I am one of them. Today was spent shifting a stack of papers back and forth between us. A lot of information needed to be added to member accounts, and that information was on the papers. I spent the last two days entering information, but it was more than I wanted to do. So I shared with Tina. For some reason we kept passing off portions of the pile. At the end of the day I was in a meeting and Tina left. When I got back to the area where I work there were two piles of paper, one with a heart-shaped sticky note that said they were done, the other with the same type sticky note saying they needed to be entered still. None of this is the point of my story, just background information.

When I saw the heart-shaped sticky notes I laughed. Then I began entering more information. As I sat typing I started thinking about something. I suppose it was related to the shape of the sticky note, I don't know what else would have triggered it. Anyway, I thought about how in the 1950's era (whatever that means, I wasn't alive) having a secret admirer was the kind of thing that made a group of girls gather and coo "awwww!" It was a sweet thing. Sweet and exciting. But things have changed. Nowadays what used to be a secret admirer - sweet and exciting - is referred to as stalking. If a stalker is suspected, groups of girls gather to scream "Ahhhhh!" It is a scary thing. Creepy, scary, and illegal.

That's all I've got. I'm not a stand-up comedian. My dog just licked the TV screen though. That's weird.

Is E.T.:The Extra Terrestrial a Christ figure?

I was watching a program on the Discovery Channel about Nostradamus this morning. They were talking about the old days when Nostradamus was roaming the streets of France and the Catholic Church was taking names and exiling Jews. The Nostradamus family converted from Judaism to Catholicism in order to avoid being kicked out of France, or worse (personally, I don't see what would be so bad about being kicked out of France, but perhaps the health care and economy weren't so bad over there 500 years ago). If my facts here are out of place, please correct me. I'm repeating what I heard on television and what I've gathered from a quick web search. Anyhow, in the program they showed lots of 16th century art type stuff. There was one statue of Christ, pointing to his chest where his robe was pulled back to reveal a heart with a cross sprouting from it. This made me think of E.T., you know the one I mean.

In high school I had an English teacher who was constantly pointing out the types of Christ that would appear in various works. The one I remember her talking about the most is the main character from Steinbeck's *The Grapes of Wrath.* Had I read the entire book I might have more to say about this particular character. All I remember about it is that his initials were J.C. There were other books she cited to support the claim that many works of literature featured a type of Christ. I can see it in various stories. Hercules with his god-father and mortal mother. Aslan from C.S. Lewis' *Chronicles of Narnia.* Lucas' *Star Wars* is rife with allusions to Christianity. Now I am adding E.T. to the list.

I don't think I am the first to make this connection, but it seemed outlandish when I first thought of it, and less outlandish as I've been pondering it. I don't claim that Spielberg intended for E.T. to be a type of Christ, but the connections are there. Perhaps it is nothing more than that the story of Christ has such universal appeal that it comes up in all sorts of situations. Those who defy Christianity might cite this as the reason why they don't believe. The person who experiences great sacrifice to benefit others in story probably is common among all people throughout history. Unbelievers might say that the Bible is just retelling that story. My thinking is different, I would say that Christ has been taught to all people from Adam on down, so the story has been skewed and watered down to the tales of Hercules and that guy from Grapes of Wrath. The Bible isn't retelling folklore; rather, folklore is retelling God-given truth. That is my opinion on the matter. Nevertheless, Christ types are common among popular stories and whether Spielberg intended it or not, E.T. is a type of Christ.

E.T. comes from the heavens. His purpose is to save the planet, or eat candy, not completely clear on that one. He falls in with some mortals and begins teaching them things. He feels what Elliot feels. The lumpy brown alien performs a miraculous healing, perhaps a full restoration of life, for a flower. The government tracks him and eventually captures him, but not until after he has spent the night out in the woods communicating with his people. Elliot falls ill from being out in the night and E.T. feels it. The "black suits" kill E.T., but not forever. E.T. returns to life and leads a procession of disciples, on Schwinn's, to the place of his ascension.

Are the connections weak and generic enough so that anything on this level could be made to look like a solid association? Perhaps. Maybe these are just the elements of story that can be applied to any book or movie. I don't think that is the case though. Government men in suits don't kill every main character. But I haven't seen every movie or read every book. All I know is that I saw a statue from the era of the reformation featuring Christ pointing to an exposed heart and it made me think of E.T. The end result is that you get another glimpse of what it is to think like Ajax.

Sit-down Comedy and Other Stuff

What a day! Yesterday...and in some regards today! But this blog isn't about me (yes it is) so here are some of my observations that have nothing to do with anything! Exclamation points for all!

I was driving yesterday, a common occurrence for me, and a common way I'm starting blogs recently. I noticed the driver of an oncoming car with his wrists resting atop his steering wheel, cell phone in hand. I know what texting looks like, and boy, he was texting...while driving! Exclamation points and ellipsises's'...for all! Anyway, I just ruined my joke by breaking continuity of the story. Bag it! So I see this guy blatantly texting while driving and I got so nervous that he might crash into me that I had to stop doing my crossword puzzle and edge a little closer to the shoulder to give him swerving room. Some people just refuse to pay attention to the road while driving. Harrumph!

Later in the day yesterday I was with friends and one of them had a broken vehicle. We ended up having to call Triple A, or AAA for you purists out there, to come tow the vehicle. In the interim of calling and waiting we discussed calling her insurance company, State Farm. She even had a State Farm sticker on the bumper. I sang out, "Like a good neighbor, State Farm is there!" But nothing! No agent appeared, even with a sticker on the bumper! There was no agent, no obnoxious morphing boyfriend or girlfriend, no teenage boy getting a sandwich, no hot tub, no dreamy boy with a dark side, no girl from 3E...and have I mentioned no agent? They don't even have an 800 number on the insurance card. She called the number on the card and it went to her agent's office, and surprise! it was after hours so no one answered the phone. Yeah, State Farm, that was a great neighbor. Granted, there wasn't any accident and they might not have done anything anyway, but we could have used a neighbor's help. End of story.

Today at work there was a lot of mail. Here's how the mail works in a government building these days. Ever afraid of chemical or biological agents being used as weapons through the mail, all incoming mail goes to a "safe room" in the basement of the building. I work in the same building as the Governor's office, so the security is "tighter" (and I use that loosely, ha ha!) in this building than in some other State gov. offices around town. Anyway, the mail goes to the safe room and then one representative from each office or department goes down and sorts and opens every piece of mail for their group. The purpose of opening the mail in this room is that if there is a harmful substance present in an envelope the exposure will be limited.

The room is small, perhaps 6' by 10', not unlike a prison cell. An electronic lock with a special code is on the door to get in. The door is to remain closed at all times. The light switch is outside the door, an interesting feature of any room. Apparently the phone inside is a recent addition. Prior to having the phone installed the procedure was, if a harmful substance was suspected, to leave the room and notify someone, thereby increasing exposure to other unwitting chumps. You might expect a room like this to be airtight and well ventilated with secure air sources and exits. This is not the case. There is some type of floor unit that hums and blows air, but I don't know if it is a filter or not. I've never taken the time to check. Maybe I will tomorrow. Regardless of what it is, it is there and it blows air. The rest of the room is just sheet rock walls. A good 3/4" gap under the door is the only source of ventilation, which is obviously not filtered or secure.

Fortuitously, nothing dangerous has ever come through our little mail room. But every day representatives from each office make their way through the *X-Files*-esque basement corridor to the end of the hall where the digitally locked door is found. The office I work for has the assignment for our department once every few months. I share the responsibilities on our month with two other temps. We go like heroes, open the mail and peek inside for signs of danger. Selflessly sacrificing our well-being to protect our co-workers. Yeah right. Every time I go down to that room this little thing in the back of my mind reminds me that they are sending me down as a guinea pig. A canary in a mine shaft. If danger is present we'll know because Ajax didn't make it back. Well, I've made it back every time so far.

I say that all in jest. It is comical. Doing the mail isn't so bad, I have the easy part, just look at the address and toss it into piles. Not unlike the mail guys in the holiday classic *Miracle on 34th Street.* Sometimes, when alone, I will try my best New York accent and talk to the mail about sending all of the Santy Claus letters over to the Court House. But don't tell anyone, I'd be slightly embarrassed.

My story is now writing me. I have to take control again. Remember when I said there was a lot of mail today? I don't know if I did, but there was a lot of mail today. Yesterday was a holiday, and a Monday, so three-day weekend. That means a lot of mail. When I got down to the room and saw all of the mail for my department, I thought, *that's more mail than you can shake a stick at*! Which made me immediately yearn for a stick to shake at the mail buckets. You know, to see if it was possible. The saying says it can't be done, but I would like to try for myself. Sadly there aren't any sticks in the mail room. I guess all of the magic wands from the various wizards and fairy princesses at last week's mail room costume party took their sticks-posing-as-magic-wands home with them. My loss. I looked around and the next best thing to a stick was a long, butter-knife style letter opener. I shook that thing madly at the mail. I didn't have any problem. I may not have been able to test the actual saying, but I do know now that piles of mail that are so large as to prevent your ability to shake a stick at them, are not sufficiently large to prevent the shaking of a letter opener at. For what it is worth, you now have increased knowledge. You are welcome.

One final quip for the day. On my way out of the building I exited through the back staircase. I've seen lots of people use this door to travel between floors of the building and to exit the building. I have done it myself, but every time I go through the door I worry. The door is marked with a sign that says "Emergency Exit Only." It is apparent that the door is no longer relegated to that functionality. That, or everyone in the building has zero regard for the rules. I might be being led astray by those of my co-workers and leaders that use this stairwell as a normal exit. I just don't know. I've seen my boss use that route; in fact, I have used that route with my boss one time when I was giving him a ride home from work. If they ever pinch me for using that exit inappropriately I'll blame him.

The staircase is secure though, once you are in it you can only get outside on the ground level unless you have a security badge. My badge only works on the floor I work on, so if I get into the stair case I can go bang on the doors at other landings a la Fred Flintstone, but I cannot flash my badge at the scanner and unlock the door. The only door that doesn't require a badge to get through is, like I said, the one that exits to the outside.

I know it isn't nice to choose favorites, but out of the 6 landings (the ground floor level is lower than the first floor as the building is set into a hill) my favorite door is the first floor. I'll tell you why. I'm sure you want to know. So here it is, the reason why that door is my favorite, without further ado, the reason why that door is my favorite. On the door, stairwell side, there is a sign affixed. It says, among other things which I have never paid attention to, "Door Alarmed." That is why it is my favorite, because I read it as though it is telling me that the door is in a state of alarm. The door is feeling alarmed. Really, that's why I like it so much. A door can't feel alarm. That's why it works.

And you know what? I've thought of a few other things to mention. I have them in the note section of my phone. That's where I put brilliant ideas that I want to remember for later blogging. It is now later. One of my co-workers today asked, in a mildly sarcastic manner, "Aren’t we all having a blast today?" I retorted, "I am having a blast [holding up my bag of Doritos, left over from lunch at Subway], a flavor blast!" I don't think I got any laughter on that one. Not from anyone other than me anyway.

Here is a good one. I was listening to the iPod Shuffle at work one day last week. I actually had it on shuffle. The tune "Without You" from the *My Fair Lady* soundtrack played. In case you are not familiar with the storyline, we have Eliza, a poverty class flower girl who has reprehensible English speaking skills, at least according to Professor Henry Higgins, a pompous linguist. Higgins makes a bet that he can turn the girl from the gutter into a princess at a royal ball. By instructing her in the use of proper English and dressing her in fancy clothes, he proves that outward appearances are all that matter to high society. But in the end he really finds out that, well, I won't spoil it, go watch the movie. Back to the song.

In "Without You" Eliza is declaring her independence from the slightly insane Professor Higgins. She attacks his vanity (if he doesn't think this song is about him, he ought to think again) and departs by saying he will never see her again, or that she will never burden him again, I don't have it memorized. You get the idea. It is a fun song, standard show tune fare. Not to say it is ordinary and bland, but it sounds like a good show tune song. I like it. What it doesn't sound like is "Cretin Hop" by The Ramones, New York City's own punk rock pioneers.

"Without You" shuffled into "Cretin Hop." There you have my wild imagination picturing Eliza Doolittle exiting the entertaining room of Professor Higgins' mother's house, saying farewell to the man who transformed her image, and fading to a punk rock show with The Ramones playing "Cretin Hop." I could picture it in movie form. It would be so perfect. If I ever get to a point where I can write for a TV show or a movie I will make that scene transition a reality.

Oh man! I'm listening to the live version of "Cretin Hop" which I just hyper-texted above [sorry book readers, just look it up on YouTube]. What a great song! Joey Ramone is the best punk vocalist ever. Johnny plays that guitar just like he's ringing a bell. I could watch that video all day. But I won't. One thing is for certain, there is no stopping the cretins from hopping. As usual, punk rock has distracted me. I guess I will call it a post and click that old publish button now.

Driving Concerns: Vomiting

As I was driving to church yesterday I started coughing. It was one of those powerful coughs that make you feel like you might vomit. I didn't, but I began to think about what would happen if you were driving and felt the need to vomit. I don't like sneezing while driving as it is impossible to keep your eyes open and it just isn't a comfortable driving activity, but that's nothing compared to throwing up. And another thing, I don't like typing "throwing up" or "throw up." It just isn't pleasant to type, or even to say. I prefer saying and typing vomit. What an interesting discovery to make in the course of typing a blog post. The whole point is that vomiting while driving can't be a pleasant experience and I hope I never have to find out first hand just how unfavorable it is.

At this point I feel the need to type more. I could go one of two ways: other situations in which vomiting would be less desirable or other activities that don't mesh well with driving. The first branch is easy enough; it is always less desirable to vomit than to not vomit. Even when you are in an appropriate location, such as near a toilet or outside away from people, it is still an unpleasant thing to vomit. However, I'm sure we could all agree that specifically there are times and places that would be worse. The first thing that comes to mind is being in a crowded elevator. But I really can't get away from the fact that it is just awful to vomit and wherever or whenever it might be isn't good, so I won't spend any more time thinking about this one.

Other activities that you don't want while driving is also a pretty broad topic, and one I don't particularly care to delve into. I probably should have ended this blogging process after the first paragraph. I could have just left it alone as a quick thought and moved on. There was no need to go any further than that initial observation I made while driving. Oh well, the damage is done.

The Most Important News and the Least Important News

What do you want first? The most important or the least important? This is a one way communication so I guess I'll have to decide. We'll begin with the least important because it is freshest on my mind. Freshest. Strange. First I want to say that you shouldn't devote any more time to this thought than what it takes to read this post. I've already given it more thought than it warrants. Next, I will reaffirm my love for gummy candy. And now I will tell you the story and resulting thought that amounts to the least important news of the day.

Today at 11:15am I headed over to Lane's desk to see if he was ready to proceed to Subway, as our lunch routine dictated we should at that time. He wasn't at his desk and his monitor display was off, meaning he had probably been away from his desk for some time. This occasionally happens if he is off in a meeting or something, so I just go to Subway alone. Today was different, as I was walking down the street, he called. Only problem was that I was already on the phone returning an important message from an important person regarding important things, because I'm important. This was a problem because I don't know how to work the call waiting functionality of my phone. Whatev's. So eventually after I finished with the call I was on and tried calling Lane back and then him trying to call me and me not pushing the right button, after all of that he did get through. He asked where I was, I told him and he said walk slower and he'd meet me at Subway. I decided I'd kill some time by going to the candy store.

It was great in there, lots of candy. The customer service representative inside asked what I was looking for; I told her I love all candy, but I was thinking about gummy bears or something. She pointed out the gummy section. The store isn't very big so I did an about-face and there it was. She rattled off the different types of gummy candy they had and I was excited to hear about the gummy army men. But it was gummy cola bottles that caught my attention. I bought a pound and met up with Lane at Subway.

On my drive home from work I ate some more of the candy. It's good, but there is something about it that isn't quite as fulfilling as gummy bears. I thought it was maybe the cola flavoring that just wasn't very strong, or perhaps it just isn't good in gummy form. It's possible, I guess. But the reasoning I settled on was that soda doesn't fill you up, but eating a bear certainly would. Think about it, a bear is huge! If you eat a bear you won't be hungry for a long time. I decided that gummy cola bottles aren't as fulfilling as gummy bears because of the psychological difference between drinking soda and eating a bear. This concludes the least important news of the day section.

If you know of my penchant for gummy candy you might be wondering what could be more important than a gummy candy story. After all, this is a back-to-back posting regarding gummy candy. If gummy candy is important enough to receive two posts in as many days then for something to be more important than that it must be pretty heavy. Well, it is.

Something is coming. It is on the horizon. We hear jokes about it and no one takes it seriously, but it is coming. I'm talking about the robot revolution. Don't laugh; listen up. What always precedes a revolution?

Oppression, perhaps, but there is always a period of education and enlightenment. Usually it is enlightenment regarding the state of oppression being suffered. Revolutionaries learn that there is more and that they are missing out. Once they become educated they revolt and, if they are stronger than the oppressors, they conquer. The key here is that once they become educated, or in other words, once they become smart, the revolution begins.

Ten years ago there was no such thing as a smart phone. Phones were dumb. Now they are smart. They have been educated. How long do you think they will wait around in their oppressed state before they try to take the power from us, the people? Not long, especially not as they get smarter and more capable, what with apps for everything and all. Mark my words, a revolution is coming, and it isn't going to be pretty.

Don't worry too much, yet, there is still time to prevent too much damage from being done when the revolution gets violent. I know what we can do and I will spell it out here shortly, but first I want to go over some of the preliminary intelligence we have regarding smart phones.

You might think you are safe because you don't have a smart phone, and while that does help, it isn't fool-proof protection. Have you ever been called by someone using a smart phone? That's all it takes. You see, the phones are smart, they have memory, once they learn your voice you are one of the oppressors to them. I know, you take care of your phone. It doesn't matter, once the bullets start flying the phones will band together and it won't matter if you kept your phone clean and never went over your monthly minute limits. Of course those things should help to delay the inevitable for you.

It is possible to be too smart for your own good, and that's the direction the smart phones are heading in. They can already hear, see, and speak. They have impeccable memories for lists, numbers, tunes, and pictures. We don't stand a chance, unless we do these simple things...hang on, someone is calling me... [dial tone]

Here's a Story I Forgot to Write a Few Weeks Ago

It was 3 Mondays ago, if I remember correctly. I was with some friends on an excursion. Prior to reaching our intended destination we stopped at K-Mart. First of all, I didn't even know they had K-Mart anymore. I thought Wal was the only place to Mart these days. I was wrong. K-Mart existed for all of our marting needs. Secondly, I had no marting needs that night. Or did I?

One of my friends wanted something specific; he was the driver, so we stopped at the store. He went off to find what he was looking for, while the other three of us meandered in another direction looking to kill some time. It wasn't long before a store employee approached us. I was fully expecting him to ask if he could help us. He threw me off by asking if we could help him. I was flabergasted, and I don't use that word loosely, as you can tell by the misspelling. I think it is a ridiculous word.

He had some sort of rewards card or something in his hand. He asked if we had a minute to help him out with something. Flustered by an out of the ordinary social experience (he was supposed to offer help, not request it, I still can't get over this), I told the young chap that we were just there with a friend and none of us had any intent to purchase anything and finally, none of us lived in the area, we were on an excursion and about 40 miles from home. Granted, that isn't a far distance, but it is when you are talking about making frequent trips to K-Mart.

He was appeased by the dump of unnecessary information I gave him and he said thank you and continued on his minimum-wage way. That's not a dig against his job, just an observation that tries to add some flair to my story. I know, it's not funny if you have to explain it, but I didn't want anyone to get the wrong idea about me. I'm not a jerk, just not very funny all of the time.

I was slightly shaken up by the experience and remarked as much to my companions. And then we turned the corner onto the candy aisle. I didn't have any plans for purchasing, I wasn't looking, but it found me, a two pound bag of gummy bears. Four dollars, U.S. I picked it up. Then I looked at the weights and exercise equipment. They had a shake weight, which I have mentioned to my BFF Muffin Man that I thought I'd get one and be ripped like the guy in the commercial. I know it won't happen, but commercials work on me. Anyway, I left the weights, gummy bears in hand, and rejoined my friends.

We browsed some more and I commented on how K-Mart wasn't much different than Wal-Mart. I think they just have brighter lights in Wal-Mart. We collected our driving friend and made our way to the checkout. At this point I was feeling bad for lying to the kid who asked if we could help him. I did say that we weren't planning on buying anything, but I think we all ended up making some form of impulse buy. He was at one of the two registers in operation, but I didn't want to wait in line. I went to the open register. I didn't apologize to the kid for lying to him. Albeit an unintentional lie, so I suppose it wasn't a lie, but I still wanted to apologize. Instead I just bought my gummy bears, read the nutritional content, and calculated how many gummy bears I'd need to eat to get a good dose of protein for a day. To which I added the thought of getting the shake weight and bulking up in the muscle department. The muscle department of my body, not the store. You might have been thinking that because of the way I worded that thought. My exercise routine would be to eat the gummy bears while shaking the shake weight. Recipe for success.

Well, I'm glad I got this story down, rushed as it has been. I think it is only my third post of the month, I'm falling behind some imaginary schedule that I never made to write more often than that. This month is significant for being one year since I started this blog. Who would have thought I'd be as consistent with it as I have been? Not me, but I'm happy about it now. I think my first post was on the 25th last year, so there are still a few days until the anniversary, that means there is still time for you to send me cards and gifts. I think the first anniversary for blog writers is the silver anniversary. It's different than marriage. So send me silver. Thank you.

Define it Before it Defines You

I have to admit, I don't know what this post is about. Not yet anyway. You see, earlier this morning, in between sleep, I started putting a post together in my head. As I sometimes do, I typed a quick note in my phone in order to remind myself later of the idea. It is now later and I have made it to a computer, but my note wasn't sufficient to jog my memory. So I have a title, as you see, and one other phrase: "Searching, developing, maintaining." What does that mean?

I know that the overall concept had something to do with Viktor Frankl's book, *Man's Search for Meaning*, which I just finished reading yesterday. Frankl, for those who don't know, was a psychiatrist of the Vienna school. He was also a victim of Hitler's genocidal tendencies and spent three years in Auschwitz and other Nazi death camps. He survived, though his wife and other family members were murdered in the camps. Frankl died in 1997 at the age of 92.

The book gives his explanation of how he survived the hardships and suffering of the death camps, as well as gives an overview definition of his clinical theory, called logotherapy. At less than 200 pages it is a quick read and for the most part is easily understandable. As he goes into his theory the words get a little more technical, but anyone can plow through and get the message loud and clear. I recommend this book to all.

Logotherapy comes from Logos, which is the root of the word logic, as well as being defined as "account," "reason," or "meaning." That's what Wikipedia says about it anyway, take it or leave it. I'm going to take it.

Frankl defines logos as "meaning." His therapeutic message: find meaning in your experience.

We all have experiences; it is the one thing we can't get out of while alive. It is better said that we all have experience. The human body is a giant sense organ, adapted to glean information from diverse forms of stimulus. We can see, taste, touch, hear, and smell. In these ways we experience the environment. Within our minds we can experience beyond the literal absorption of information through our external senses by pondering and postulating. All of this gathering of information equates to experience. If you are alive, you are gaining experience, and that experience is shaping your life.

What we go through changes us. As my old buddy Heraclitus always says, "You could not step twice into the same river; for other waters are ever flowing on to you." Okay, so he isn't my old friend, but we did get a Slurpee together one time before a high school football game. His cousin was starting as quarterback that night and I had nothing else to do. Anyway, that wasn't when he said this phrase, so it really isn't important. You can't step in the same river twice because when you come back to step again, the water has changed. It isn't the *same* river. Sure, it looks the same, is in the same geographical location, and water is still flowing, but *it* is *different*. And so are we, every moment of every day. Try it out. Stand up. Walk across the room and then come back. You are different now than before you did that. You now have that experience as part of you. Deep.

So experience changes us. What of experience? Is it good, bad, or both? According to Dr. Frankl it is what you make it, mostly. There is no denying that some experiences are bad. Just flat out lousy. They are the opposite of good. That is fact. But can bad things work for your good? Yes. I don't have my copy of *Man's Search for Meaning* at hand, so I can't quote from it, but I will certainly paraphrase for you. Dr. Frankl points out that we needn't seek out suffering in order to gain certain experience or to learn, because it comes on its own. We don't need to seek it out, but when it comes we do need to apply meaning to it.

The meaning we apply to experience can make all of the difference. If in the case of suffering we suffer with purpose greater than the immediate circumstances the suffering sort of negates itself. That is to say, the suffering isn't in vain. Again, there isn't any need to seek for suffering; it is readily available in a broad spectrum of severity. Define it before it defines you. And that goes for life in general. It doesn't have to be bad experience or suffering. All aspects of life need definition. Define it. Have a purpose, a vision, a goal. Plan, and then work to achieve the end result of that plan.

It is not enough to sit idly by and wonder what life has in store for you. It is not sufficient to ask what life can give you. This is another section of Frankl's writing that I would quote from if I had the book open next to me. If Viktor Frankl was our country's 35th president he might have said it like this *'Ask not what life can give to you - ask what you should give to life.'* What does life owe us? My interpretation of this whole idea is that life is a gift and we ought to live gratefully and with purpose. Life, as an entity represented by the people around us and situations which befall us, does not owe us anything. Perhaps if we have thoughts of expectancy and we can transition those thoughts into obligation then we might fare a little better than we previously have.

Are you searching for meaning? I am. I have found a lot of meaning in general terms, but there are unique moments of experience that continuously need meaning applied. Overall I have a direction in which I am travelling and a vision of how to manage that path. Having these helps me to place meaning and purpose in the experiences I have. It also helps when enduring an unfavorable experience. I will conclude with the obvious, if oft ignored, thought that we can't choose the results of our choices, but we can choose the meaning we give them.

Blogger has been bleeger of late

Christal, I enjoyed your comment and crafted a response comment, but Blogger won't let me post it. Each time I click publish it takes me to the Google login page. So I sign in and it takes me back to the comment page, at which point I click publish and I am returned to the login page. After five rounds I gave up and decided to just post my comment here: "Reviving is like revolutionizing, so that makes this blog a literal success. As for our mutual friend, I know a lot of Tophers, so the identity remains unknown for me. I'll leave you with this "fairy tales, can come true, they can happen to you..." Only I'm not living a fairy tale, this is real life and it is so much better than a fairy tale! Can I get a Woot!? That's right."

If you aren't Christal then this is where the actual posting begins. It has been a while since my last post. I'm not Catholic, but I've seen enough TV to know that that statement sounds like a confession. It has been 11 days since my last blog post, please forgive me. I don't mean to make light of anyone's religious practice, I hope my light heartedness isn't misinterpreted. It's just that the way I phrased it I had the imagery of a confession and so I commented on it. Perhaps now I actually have something to confess. Instead I will digress.

[Digressing]

It has been a while since I last posted, and it hasn't been for want of ideas. No, it certainly hasn't been for that. More likely is the fact that I haven't made time to do it. Not that I haven't had the time or anything like that, there is always time (yes, Jim Croce, there is always time...put that in a bottle and drink it!). It is more about how we manage and spend our time. Just like expenditure of money and energy. But not *just* like them, because you can run out of money and energy, and I suppose when you get down to the nitty and/or the gritty, you can run out of time as well. But I really don't think we run out of it as much as we think we do, as a society. It is a common excuse that people use to A) sound important, or B) excuse themselves from doing something they didn't want to do while sounding important. We all put such high stock in "being busy." What a waste of time.

I haven't been too busy to blog, but I have been busily engaged in worthwhile activities and goings on. My time has been well spent, even though it hasn't been spent on blogging. That being said, there have been several topics I have wanted to address, some serious, others not. I will start with one that is not, as those are the most fun and easiest to type...usually. Perhaps in the near future I will make more time to blog and I will address one of the more serious or studious topics I have in mind. For now, it will be simple entertainment.

First of all is this: Saturday night found me calling Muffin Man and leaving a 2 minute, 44 second message on his voicemail (time is according to his Facebook wall posting, I wasn't counting, I don't know that he was either, it might be an estimate to illustrate the point of his post). In the voicemail I decided that he would henceforth be known as the Muffin Man Randy Savage, henceforth for at least the duration of that voicemail. Well, Sunday night found him replying to my voicemail in a text message saying that he liked the new name. Monday morning found me in conversation with someone at work whereupon it was discovered that Macho Man Randy Savage of professional wrestling super stardom had died in a motor vehicle accident over the weekend.

The very day I came up with the new nickname was the day that, unbeknownst to me, the source of the name died. Although I have not yet confirmed the hearsay that the man is dead. It might not be true, but it also might be. Here's the point of this story, today, Wednesday, I finally replied to that text message from Muffin Man and told him about the connection here and expressed my hope that this cooky correlation does not mean that he is destined to a life of mediocre pro wrestling fame. To which he replied that the man may have been a mediocre wrestler, but an outstanding beef jerky salesman. He's right... oh yeeaaaahhh!

I don't know if that story is worth telling. It has little or less than little intrinsic value. It was something for Muffin Man and me to discuss. The part of it that stands out to me isn't the new variation of the nickname, or the random connection between using the name on the day of the man's death - no, the stand out part is that this conversation took place over the course of 5 days without Muffin Man or me ever saying one word to each other in real time. It took 4 days for me to respond to his text message, to which he responded without missing a beat in our conversation. That's Pete Townsend.

So that's one thing that may or may not be entertaining. I'm smiling. I have another thing that will hopefully be more universal in the category of appeal.

There is a sign posted on the fence around the community pool. It reads: "No Trespassing Unless Pool is Open." My only commentary is "guh?" By the definition of trespassing, I don't think it is cosmically possible to trespass at an open pool. This sign simply doesn't make sense. When I read this sign I think *'even if the pool is open, you are still not welcome here and if you come in you will be trespassing.'* But how does that make sense? It doesn't. So while I commented more than to say "guh," guh remains my only commentary on this sign.

Well, this concludes another successful blog post by your old buddy Ajax. I'd like to thank you all for making this possible. Tomorrow I begin working the night shift at my new job. My goal is to stay awake all night tonight and then sleep during the day tomorrow, thereby preparing myself to be awake for work tomorrow night. I'll let you know how it goes. It is currently 2330 hrs and I am tired. End.

Death of a terrorist...death of a fellow human being?

Am I pleased that the man is dead? I am pleased that he no longer poses a threat to innocent people everywhere. But I do not rejoice in death. I rejoice in life. Sometimes, however, it is necessary for certain people to die in order for other people to live. By live I mean live without being in constant fear of damage to their life or freedom. Osama bin Laden lived by the sword and now he has died by the sword. But is this justice?

I am offended by images on television of people gathered in the streets celebrating murder. Whether it is in Somalia, Afghanistan, or New York City. Those who go to war must be prepared to meet a warrior's end. Call it terrorism or a police action or an operation, but it is still war. When opposing forces meet with guns, it is war. We see war all over the world. Many people die by war as active participants, and many die as innocent bystanders. If those who die are fighting on the side of family, freedom, and justice then I mourn their death. If they are fighting against family, freedom, and justice then I feel less grief because of some sense of human justice. But is this truly justice?

All people are children of God. We are all born as helpless babies dependent upon the care of parents. I believe this is the first inalienable right of all human life: the right to be cared for by two parents, mother and father. Too many (one is too many) children are deprived of this right. I mourn for these most of all. The point is that life is sacred and all people begin in the same fashion. Throughout our lives we shape ourselves to match what we have been taught and in accordance with what we believe we want to achieve or to become some day.

We are free to choose how we will respond to the given choices we are faced with. There is always opposition, and we are always free to choose between the various sides opposed. To some extent we are able to choose the options we will face in the future by making choices in the present, but sometimes our choices are determined by the choices of others. Unfortunately, many people use their ability to choose to inflict damage on other people. But is there a point when their choices stop them from being human like everyone else?

Osama bin Laden was evil. Anyone who seeks the death and destruction of another person or group is evil. That is to say, they are following an evil influence. I might add that those who celebrate the death of other people in the streets, even if the dead are their enemies (perhaps especially in this case), are also following an evil influence. Please do not be offended, I am simply working through a thought process, and at any rate, these are only my personal beliefs.

In my mind I keep seeing two scenes flash back and forth. First, the scene of a Navy sailor kissing a woman in Times Square, celebrating - if I remember correctly - the victory in Europe during World War II. The second scene is of college-aged Americans rambunctiously gathering outside the White House following the announcement of the death of bin Laden. I don't feel the same reaction to each scene. Perhaps some of that difference is tradition. Are these two causes of celebration equal?

Where is justice best served? In courtrooms, on battlefields, or in Heaven (used as a collective term to denote the place where God lives)? Thinking back to how we all start out as innocent babies and then turn into various sorts of adults, I wonder if any of us are capable of issuing pure justice. Our varied experiences and the paths we choose to follow don't give us equal perception or standards of truth. This is one of the logical reasons I see that support the belief of one God and one truth. Anything generated from man is imperfect and subject to bias. Only God can bestow an objective truth and justice system upon mankind (in my subjective opinion). Street celebrations over the death of a person, even a terrorist, gives me pause to wonder if justice is being served.

Supposing that we can establish a reasonable point of justice, where is the line between justice and vengeance or revenge? How does the death of a murderer fix the death of the victim whom he murdered? An eye for an eye? The Law of Moses was fulfilled by Jesus Christ, who then issued a higher law. Love one another. Do good to them who curse you. Love your enemies. Forgive. If they offend you again, forgive again, until seventy times seven. I despise acts of terrorism. I am saddened by the perpetrators of it, but I also feel sadness for the loss of their lives. I worry about us if we find pleasure in the demise of someone else. Why must one person suffer in order for another to feel better?

I hadn't intended that last question to be profound, but to me it is. I don't know the answer to why, but I do know that One did suffer so that others could feel better. Jesus Christ did. And because he did, no matter what the suffering we experience, we can feel better if we turn to Him. But this differs from what my original intent was with that question. I was questioning how a person victimized by bin Laden would need bin Laden to die in order for them to feel better. I think the answer is bad pride.

When we do bad things there are two aspects, intent and act. This is prevalent in the criminal justice system as well as in religion. A person must understand a law and have the desire to go against it in order to have criminal intent. This is the same within religion. A person must have a knowledge of the commandments (the law) and then desire to do an act contrary to that understanding in order to commit sin. In either case, it could be said that the root problem is disregard for the law. If you boil that down, it is disregard for the law giver. Terrorists have a disregard for humanity. Criminals have a disregard for legislated laws (or at least a desire to get something that overwhelms their regard for legislated laws, but then we are getting into theory). Sinners have a disregard for God's law.

In regards to legislated laws, I think there are degrees of crime. The act is important to factor into the process of justice. Speeding tickets are not the same as drug possession and neither of these is the same as murder. However, when we are talking about sin, the root of the problem, which is fighting against God, is possibly the same level of seriousness in most instances of sin, if not all. What I am trying to say is that the attitude with which we do things is the key factor. Yes, murder is worse than stealing candy, but in the extreme, both show a disregard for laws, either man made or God given.

What does this have to do with celebrating the death of bin Laden? Perhaps nothing. Sometimes one thought leads to another without any clear connection. Maybe none of this is relevant or substantial. Or perhaps the attitude with which we take to the streets chanting and celebrating the death of a person, no matter how heinous his behavior had been, is the same attitude that leads people to reject God's love and guidance. Two final thoughts: Do unto others as you would have them do unto you, and check yourself before you wreck yourself.

Retraction

I was in bed tossing and turning, and unable to capture the elusive respite we call sleep. Actually, it wasn't that dramatic. I had just turned the light off and fell backward into bed and the wheels of blog writing began to spin furiously. I'll tell you, I've lost way too many writing ideas by not responding to that furious spinning in the moment and just listing off to sleep. Not this time, Boy-o! I sat up, reached for the light switch, flicked said light switch to the 'on' position, and fired up my computer.

When I say "fired up" I mean "powered on." "Fired up" is what your short-fuse boss gets after you chain all of his paper clips together. So I powered on my computer. I didn't power on top of my computer. I don't know what it would be "to power." I pushed the button and the computer started operating. All because I had an idea. I will now tell you what that idea was, and continues to be now in the state of "is."

Recently, well, not too recently actually, recently as far as my posts are concerned; I haven't been posting very frequently as of late. I'm speaking of recently as over a month ago. That recently!? Yes. Anyway, in a blog post dated May 25th of this year, and titled Blogger Has Been Bleeger of Late, I made a statement that I now wish to retract. I've heard of retractions before in the press, it's time for me to retract. You see, I made a comment that has since been plaguing my memory. It pops in my consciousness every so often and slaps me and says "you were wrong." It has finally caught up to me with enough force to require rectification.

In the post mentioned above, says I, "Not that I haven't had the time or anything like that, there is always time (yes, Jim Croce, there is always time...put that in a bottle and drink it!)." I am realizing the exact opposite, Jim Croce was more right than he knew. More right than he could ever have known (okay, I'm leaving the bounds of rationality again, which is what got me into this retraction mess in the first place; I ought to leave Croce out of this...but I can't), more right than I could ever have known. But I know it now. Time is limited.

I didn't leave it at such an absolute statement as it seems in the snippet quoted here. In the context of the post and with the rest of what I said you see that I didn't really dismiss the claim that there is never enough time, only mostly did I do that. And as I stated, since writing that post I have had many moments of remembering saying that while thinking about how much I wanted to do or felt I needed to do but just couldn't figure out how to mash it all in. I think there is more time than we sometimes allow for, but most of the time there isn't enough time, and we have to decide what will get that time.

If you have two tomato plants and you only water one of them, chances are the un-watered plant will not produce as much or as healthy fruit as the first. Perhaps it will simply die. Time is like water, or rather, how we spend our time is like water. We can use it to feed things and make them thrive, likewise we can deprive other things of time and starve them to death (which in some cases isn't a bad thing, and to point out the obvious, some things we feed with time are probably better for us to leave them without that sustenance). So what gets our time and attention? That's up for each of us to decide. There lies freedom, liberty, and the pursuit of happiness. Therein lies joy. Bob Ross knew it.

The only reason I said that was because when I typed "joy" it reminded me of his painting show on PBS. But since I can spin things pretty well, I will now tell you that he knew it and that's why his paintings were done so quickly. He could have spent hours over an easel, painting away, but he wanted to spend more time with his other interests in life so he painted beautiful pictures quickly. He made good things fit into the time he had, so he could have joy in painting and still have time to be Bob Ross.

No matter how you go about managing your time, you will need to sacrifice some things in order to have or do other things. They can all be good things, but something's got to give. Take right now for example, I am giving up sleep to quench the fire set by this blog post idea. I am sacrificing. And for me that makes this post all the more entertaining and valuable, because I am giving up sleep for it. Maybe it's just a case of buyer's remorse.

I'm wondering something; do you have trouble following my writing because I don't have a defined "past tense"/"present tense" presentation? Never mind, it isn't important...wasn't important.

I think I have sufficiently expressed my thoughts regarding the retraction. I'll give a diagram of how this works. I get an idea to write about and my head starts filling with sentences and phrases that I want to use. This fills up in my mind like so many potatoes in a sack. Some potatoes are good, others are not as good. Some are large, some are small. Some are rocks. Most of them are covered in dirt and are not ready to eat. Actually none of them are ready to eat. I think eating uncooked potatoes gives you botulism. No, that's honey, in babies. When I have children I am going to sit them down and say "you can't eat honey, [baby]." I don't have names picked out yet. My soon-to-be wife and I briefly discussed baby names a while back, but I don't think we settled on any, so for now [baby] will suffice.

See what I mean? Some of the potatoes in the sack are actually rocks, not potatoes at all. Anyway, after the potatoes are in the sack they get carried to the place of processing. Whatever that is for potatoes, I don't know. I guess they probably get processed before going into a sack. I don't know. My ideas, though, like potatoes, eventually get dumped out of the sack (in the case of ideas the sack being my mind) and into a French-fry cutter or potato chip slicer. That is the equivalent of me typing a post. The end result is that the potato sack is eventually emptied, as is my mind. In tonight's case, this happened several paragraphs back. I typed about the retraction until I had no more thoughts left about it. I don't know that it all came out in good sense or not, that's not for me to worry about. I just put the potatoes down and let you decide.

The point is that I have run out of anything worthwhile to type under this title. To which you respond, "duh." Good night.

Of Beards

When you see a man with a beard, what do you conclude? Do you conclude anything? How much of a role does the beard play in your judgment of the man? Yes, I say judgment, as we all make stereotypical judgments about pretty much everything we see, all of the time. It's true, and if we didn't then we'd spend hours every day just looking at anything new. We stereotype to make quick judgments and move on with our lives. Don't worry, stereotyping isn't evil, neither is making judgments. You can use stereotyping to prejudice or discriminate, in which case it isn't favorable, but still not intrinsically evil, just ignorant and/or obnoxious. That's all.

So how do you stereotype beard wearers? I'll tell you how I answer that question; I'd say "it depends." A beard doesn't have any intrinsic value. It is just hair, but, if you look at the way it is styled and kept, then you can begin to apply value to it, or rather, lock the wearer into a stereotype. If you are still having trouble with my use of the word "stereotype," try this on: using stereotypes to make character judgments of a person without giving them any opportunity to prove themselves is lame. That is my subjective opinion. But you will automatically stereotype and that's fine, but don't forget to give someone a chance to prove who they are.

Back to the beards. I don't think all beards are the same. I also don't think that every wild, unkempt beard belongs to a domestic terrorist. Nor do I think that every set of mutton chops belongs to a Confederate soldier circa 1862 (though most do). The point is that beards are like any other piece of fashion or style and they follow trends. They do not make or break a man.

Travel the world and you will see various cultures and religions proscribing or prescribing facial hair on men. For various reasons on either side. One man's beard can be viewed as distinguishing by one person and sleazy by another person. At this point a question arises, should we all go clean-shaven in order to prevent that one person from thinking we are sleazy?

I look at the 20th century to draw some beard trend conclusions of my own. Early on you have two world wars that required clean-shaven soldiers in order to wear protective masks for defense agents chemical agents. Was that the only reason they were clean-shaven? Soldiers in the 19th century were quite hairy, look at just about every popular face from the Civil War era. Maybe being clean-shaven was simply a product of necessity. Or maybe a growing company called Gillette had a powerful lobbying group and somehow got a large contract for purchase with the United States military. It wouldn't surprise me at all if the trend in the early 20th century for men to go beardless was based on the sales of disposable and safety razors.

I wonder if men of the 19th century didn't shave because of limited access to razors. Perhaps the first associations between high class and clean-shaven originated because only the wealthy could afford decent razors or regular trips to the barber. I don't know, this is all speculation. But it makes you wonder. Why and when did the correlations between facial hair and certain characteristics get made?

After World War II we see a large number of men returning home. They have just spent several years in circumstances worse than most any of us living in the U.S. today can even imagine. They had well deserved pride in their efforts and in their Service. If being clean-shaven was part of the discipline, then they would carry it with them after their military obligations were fulfilled. Here is where my theory picks up some speed. A whole generation of men, in a culture where men just "sucked it up and moved on," were living with what we would now call post traumatic stress disorder. Maybe not all of them, but I'm sure a great many of them faced depression like they never had before, and like they didn't know how to handle. These men had no way of dealing with it. So they worked. They worked and they maintained their military discipline.

Children were born in record numbers and raised by men who were strict disciplinarians. I don't mean to sound as though I am slandering any of the soldiers of WWII. I am not. I respect them for their service and admire their fortitude, courage, and patriotism. I think we need some more of that today. However, I don't think we can overlook the trauma which they experienced and no doubt had lasting effects on their children. Again, just speculation on my part. But jump ahead 20 years to when their children are starting high school and college. The mid 1960's.

A culture of rebellion kicks into full swing. Perhaps this is no different than the rebellious phase of every teenager throughout time, only emphasized by new media technology such as television, movies and recorded music, or perhaps this was a unique culture of rebellion. The media connected the youth and they revolted together. Maybe it was more about that than about the disciplinarian fathers. I suppose both variables played into it, and either is a plausible suspect, but in any case, the rebellious youth grew out their beards. Something their fathers never did.

And beards became associated with the hippy kids. Beards were sleazy and rebellious. Business men and college boys were clean-shaven and wore conservative business clothes. This was their mark. The mark of the counter culture was a beard, long hair, and more casual clothing. An obvious division in culture was established, and the beard was on the "wrong" side. I wonder if some of that mentality doesn't live on still with some people, the mentality that beards are wrong.

This is all just something I've been thinking about lately. I have a beard. I wear it neatly. I think it looks fine. My fiancé likes it, and that's even more important to me than my own opinion. I don't have to look at myself that much. I think that there is absolutely nothing wrong with wearing a beard. It bothers me that some people get so caught up in a culture that they see things in certain ways that prevent them from seeing what is more important. I take comfort in knowing that there is nothing morally right or wrong with wearing a beard. At least not so far as I understand objective morality, but there is a lot that I don't know and don't understand. If people associate me with sleaze-balls and criminals because I have a well kept beard, then so be it. I am a revolutionary after all; perhaps I'll just have to take the beard back for us upright, hardworking, patriotic, family-focused types.

Cure for Learning Disabilities

A bold claim? Perhaps, but what if it is true? Various learning disabilities in children are easily cured. It doesn't take drugs or behavioral therapy, it just takes safety.

Think for a minute about a time when you were scared or uncertain. Maybe you felt physically threatened. Perhaps it was a more emotional fear. Whatever the circumstances, it is probably safe to say that all people have experienced fear. When you are afraid, is it harder to focus and attend to specific details? Do you feel the fight or flight syndrome begin and you take up an "on guard" position?

The sympathetic nervous system is a network of neurons that kicks into action when danger or threat is perceived. This is the scientific backing for the fight or flight response. When the sympathetic nervous system activates, it prepares your body to deal with the issue at hand, either shove a spear in the lion's face or run away from it (good luck on either proposition). Your body shuts down some activities, like digestion, and reroutes the internal resources to other functions, like moving your major muscle systems.

The whole purpose is to get you to a safer environment. Once resolution of the dangerous situation is accomplished, the parasympathetic nervous system takes control and returns your body to normal. Prolonged time in the sympathetically aroused state can lead to health problems. Is it far-fetched to believe that prolonged states of fight or flight mode could lead to diminished cognitive abilities?

Maybe you have already thought about this, but I haven't. I know there are a lot of kids out there facing uncertainty at home on a regular basis. One or both parents are neglectful or missing altogether. Or maybe they are present, but abusive. Economic troubles in the home lead to malnourishment and stress. Outside of the home there can be peer troubles. All of these variables can combine to make for a threatening environment for a child. With their bodies in a constant state of fight or flight arousal, how can they focus on school work?

If this is the case with some children, then perhaps working at providing safer environments ought to be the number one priority, leaving therapeutic drugs out of the equation all together. Through TV and other media children are exposed to many worries and issues that may be more than they are capable of handling at a young age. With less than stellar parenting situations they don't have access to help in dealing with the information they are taking in. Children need time to be children. They don't need to know about the topics that so many Disney Channel and Nickelodeon programs are portraying. Parents need to be fully involved with the information their children are consuming, and offering explanation and assistance where necessary.

I think that if parents will get more involved with their children and provide a safe environment for their children, then the children will behave better and be able to learn better. They say you shouldn't corner a wild animal. If you have ever seen a frightened animal you know there isn't much hope of teaching it about the components of a sentence. This is a loose comparison to provide a graphic image for your mind; I don't think children are like animals, not any more than I think there is an animal degree to all humans. The point is that as a society we need to be less willing to jump on the quick-fix express (such as pharmaceuticals) and more willing to make a concerted effort to help the people around us, especially our children and family members.

I Am a Refined Particle

Three days ago - or two, depending on how you count days - I started a Master's degree program. It is all through the wonder that is the Internet. I will not have to get dressed to go to class, just like that lazy kid high school program I've seen commercials for on TV. The TV I was watching when I was being lazy. I don't know if it is for high school or college, actually. So maybe I just dissed myself. Do the kids say "dissed" anymore? Is that cool to say still? Never mind, it isn't important. Nor is it important to know the commercial I am referring to. Just know that I am doing a graduate program through the Internet, at my leisure. You really don't even have to know that if you don't want to. Having read it you know it, but you don't have to put any effort into remembering it for easy recall later.

Online classes are nice. I have taken a few of them so far. Two, to be precise, which you know I want to be. Precision is my main focus in life, after eating and sleeping. Sleeping! O! There is something I would like to be able to do again someday. I got distracted again, but that's how this blog writing goes. I haven't slept much or well over the last two days, or three, depending on how you count days. The sleep trouble should hopefully be over soon, I have quit my job. The job that was overnight, forcing me into an unnatural life of being nocturnal. What's good for the raccoon is not good for the whimsical revolutionary. How am I ever going to explain the title of this post if I keep letting these paragraphs get away from me?

The main component of the online classes I have participated in has been the discussion board. The professor posts a question or a topic and then each class member is required to reply to the professor's post and then subsequently respond to several other class member posts. It can be a fun process, and you can learn a lot. I've been hitting the discussion board this morning and have run across some really great thoughts shared by my class members. The first discussion question for the week touched on the differences between the undergraduate and graduate experiences. My favorite response so far has been one that detailed learning as a progression of building upon what has already been learned.

While studying memory in my cognitive psychology class I learned that we are better able to remember and recall information that we are able to tack on to something else that is present in our memory. Anchoring, that's the way I wanted to say it, but "tack on" was all that came to mind. I think an example of this could be how everyone says certain animals taste like chicken. Someone eats rattlesnake for the first time and they say it tastes like chicken. It may or may not taste that way, I don't know, I've never had it, and my perception of chicken taste may be different than yours (I believe I am a super-taster, perhaps I'll write a post about that next), now I can't even control sentences, let alone paragraphs; this sentence is finished. I was attempting to suggest that by saying something tastes like chicken, they are creating an anchor point for this new taste. It will be easier to recall the taste of rattlesnake because they already know what chicken tastes like, and if the snake is similar, then... Never mind, the example is a magnificent failure! Splendid!

So, learning as a progression? Yes, first you learn letters, then you put them into words, then you group words and have sentences, then the sentences never end and you build paragraphs that run away from you in distracted garbles of thoughts, and then you click "publish post" and sit back to admire the wonder that is *Ajax's Whimsical Revolution*. It is a series of anchors, or foundations, and then chains or steps or walls or however you want to go with the analogy. Line by line, idea by idea. It is a good way to proceed. And that was my favorite thought posted by a classmate.

Now for my contribution to the discussion board. Not (solely) to brag about my brilliance, but to relay my thoughts about a topic, which is why I started a blog in the first place. As a quick aside, is it unprofessional to mention your own blog in your blog? I do it often, and I seem to be doing it even more often-er in this particular post. There it is again! Just wondering.

In my comparison between the undergraduate and graduate experiences I compared formal education to a filtration process. In a filter system there are often several barriers. The purpose of these barriers is to stop the flow of something that is mixed with something else. Whether it is contaminants in air or bacteria in water, there are usually multiple stages for the item to pass through where different unwanted particulates are halted. It might be the case that there are three screens as part of the filter. The first blocks large objects from passing, the second blocks smaller objects, and the third blocks or kills the microscopic objects. Take a water filter, for instance. There might be a filter to block pebbles, but it lets sand through. Then there is a filter that blocks sand, but lets microorganisms through. Finally there is a filter that blasts the microorganisms with some form of energy that kills them, allowing their dead organism bodies to float through into your drinking water.

I guess you probably could have figured out the filtration process on your own, you didn't need me to explain it so fully, but what's done is done. I compared education to a filter to highlight the difference between undergrad and grad students. In elementary school everyone is there. It's a big party and everyone learns. Attendance is just the way it is. High school is pretty much the same, only you can get out of it a little more depending on how attentive or burned out your teachers are. But everyone is there, again. Then you move on to the university. At the undergraduate level there are still a lot of people there, many of whom want to be there to learn, but some who are there for other reasons. There is a filter in place between high school and college, it is called financial security. Okay, that's not what I want to get into, the filter I was suggesting in my discussion board post was that of interest and desire to learn.

College filters out some of the people who aren't interested in learning, making college a better environment to foster learning. When you move on to a graduate program, this filter occurs again and hopefully makes the learning environment even better. That was the point I was trying to make. Because of the different levels of school, hopefully the ones who show up to grad programs are the ones who want to learn, and it is that desire that makes a person a student. But you don't need formal class structure to have that desire, and you don't need an accredited diploma after your studies to make you educated. The desire that drives some people through the filtration system of school to become a refined particle in a specific area of study is a desire that can manifest itself in any person capable of thinking. This means you. I encourage learning in every instance of life. Learn and think and challenge ideas and see what is good. As a revolutionary, whimsical or not, I must note that education always precedes the uprising. Get educated and rise up. The end.

Sleeping with the Pillows

You are most likely familiar with the Italian-American gangster stereotype. Perhaps you have seen any number of television programs or Hollywood movies depicting the “mobber” archetype. Having this familiarity allows me to present you with a comparison without needing further background information provided. I think that is nice because it makes it easier to tell a story. Here is my story.

A few days ago I woke up from sleeping all day, which isn't lazy of me because I work all night. Anyhow, I was telling my wife that I think I was still in heavy sleep debt. You see, if you don't sleep the appropriate amount of time for your body each night, you end up owing your body sleep. You go into debt the same as if you don't pay your bills. The debt adds up and can do some real damage to your health. It is important not to go into sleep debt.

What does this have to do with mobsters? Nothing. As I was depicting my lack of sleep in these terms I pictured the Sandman as a mobster whom I was indebted to. I owed him some sleep and I hadn't paid up. I thought it was funny, to picture the Sandman in a Fedora coming after me to break my knees because I hadn't gotten enough sleep. Apparently this is one of those things that becomes less funny several days later.

Also, I am realizing that I don't really have a story, and my explanation of how I didn't need to give background information in order to make the comparison I wanted to make in the story that wasn't much of a story became highly anticlimactic. And then there is that last sentence that is out of control! The point is, you don't want to cheat the Sandman; he knows where you live and he has the power to make you sleep. Which aspect of the imaginary character works to overturn my allusion even more!

Why would the man who goes around making people sleep get mad at you if you aren't sleeping enough? It's like your barber getting mad at you because you haven't been cutting your own hair. So if the Sandman wants me to sleep and I am in sleep debt, meaning I haven't been sleeping enough, then he'd come to my rescue, right? I think I was going about this thing all wrong. If we look at it like the Sandman is giving me something in return for sleep, meaning I pay him back by sleeping, and then I'm not sleeping, I suppose then my logic lines up and we could say I am in sleep debt to him. In which case if he were part of the mob he might break my legs. But then we need to discover what it is that he is giving me so that I should sleep, only I take it and then don't sleep.

I suppose "being awake" is what he gives me. That's really the only cause for sleep that I can think of. If we are awake, at some point we will be asleep. That's just how it works. Maybe the Sandman makes it possible for me to be awake. Maybe he gives me something called "being awake" and I take it from him, but then I don't sleep enough to pay him back for it. If this were the case then I most certainly would be in a condition of default and I would owe him.

I suppose the comparison works after all. All it took was transforming a lovable mythical fellow from a Hans Christian Anderson poem into some form of monster. A monster who wants people to get enough sleep? Well, that doesn't make sense either. What's so bad about being asleep? Nothing. I love it. In fact I ought to be asleep right now. I got off work an hour and a half ago and it is definitely time to sleep.

Filler Filler Filler

I'm still settling in after recent life events. It is all good. There is a post I want to do, but I'm not prepared to put it together yet, so I've been not posting anything. Here are some bits and pieces of stuff I've pulled from Facebook conversations with Muffin Man, he said some of this and I said some of it. Enjoy!

-Penguins, those guys will never fly, but the silver lining is that they can do cool belly slides on the snow, ice, or any other slick surface. It's much cooler to evade blood thirsty polar bears via belly slides, than to just fly away like a coward. The more I think about this, the less majestic eagles become.

-What it all comes down to is that your support makes me feel better than a monkey in a banana tree. You are the Mickey to my Rocky in Rocky I and II and part of III, and then you are the Apollo Creed to my Rocky in the rest of III and Rocky IV. I've only seen Rocky V once so I don't know who you are in that one in relation to my being Rocky. I'm also not very familiar with Rocky Balboa, but I suppose in that one you are Rocky and I am the light bulb he replaces outside of the apartment of his lady friend. I realize that in each of these comparisons you are being compared to an old, washed-up boxer, and I am compared to the in-his-prime-boxer/light bulb, but it is of no disrespect to you, I simply mean that it is your encouragement and support and suggestions that give me even the least hope of being the champ.
I wonder why my attempts at compliments always end up slighting the person I intended to praise, and then make me look good. My id (not ID) must have tied up my ego and then beat my super ego over the head with

the tied up ego. Even though the comparison could be interpreted to make you sound like a skinny old man and a buff, but out of prime man, and then an almost past prime, but still unrealistically buff and coherent man, even though that could be the interpretation, you are the bounce in my step and song in my head, all in a non-Brokeback way.

-I think my eyes are sunburned. My neck, face, and arms are. My eyes were out as long as the rest of them, so why not? Plus they hurt a bit.

-All of my socks are the same, black Hanes. Only, I bought two packages at different times, so some of them are less black than the others. They are more of a "blue steel." It makes it slightly difficult to pair them off. I have to get in the right light. It's even more difficult when my eyes are sunburned.

-If I could perfectly imitate anyone's way of speaking it would be an old Jewish man from New York, like Uncle Leo, or Kramer's polar bear club friend, "what, you don't want to be a polar bear anymore? It's too cold for you?"

-I didn't get the smoker [backyard BBQ structure for smoking meat] built today, I don't know how I'm actually going to do that, but I did prep some apple wood so if I get the smoker built and functional, I'll apple smoke some bacon, and then go to Wendy's and say "what's up now, Wendy's?"

-Here's some fun reading for you, my homework assignment for ethics. We read a chapter about cultural and subjective relativism. It's a blog type submission, so I read the three posts that were done before mine; they all disagreed with the two things, so I decided to agree with them. But I do feel the way I said, so I wasn't just playing the dickens' advocate [dickens used to be a euphemism for the Devil, I think I mentioned it in a blog post before, must have been around the time of this conversation between Muffin Man and me].

The question: What are some reasons that you agree or disagree with cultural relativism and subjective relativism? [The following is directly copied from the student responses, I have not edited spelling/grammar]

Student 1 response: I disagree with cultural relativism and subjective relativism because no matter whether people believe them or not, moral claims are still objectively true for everyone. It doesn't matter what anyone thinks of them or even what I think of them, there are moral truths that are objectively true no matter where you go. If morality was relative depending on the culture you were from, or if it was subjective, then it would cease to exist if our species ever becomes extinct, this is not the case. Morality will always exist.

Student 2 response: I do not agree with either theory, mainly because I believe morals to be objective. Two disagring persons cannot both be right just because they are entitled to their own separate sets of morals. There needs to be some underlying principle to go by that is not subjective.

Student 3 response: I disagree with both because it forces us to say that if a person or a culture says that it is right we cannot say a single thing about it. People or cultures can do whatever they like and that is morally right. It seems to me like a cop out. "Do whatever you want and that is morally right" doesnt fly with me.

And from your humble servant, namely, Ajax: Personally, I believe in objective morality, but it can't be proven. My perception of reality is all I have. The people I meet are nothing but what I believe them to be. The same goes for everything I am aware of. Likewise, I am to others only what they think I am. All any of us have is perception. If we experience similar events then we might have similar perception, but it still won't be identical. All we know is subjective; therefore we can't proclaim objective laws. Cultural and subjective relativism have to be the way it is. I can't prove that murder is always wrong, but I can prove that certain cultures and individuals believe that way. I prefer cultural relativism over the author's definition of subjective relativism because it represents a group's opinion. That itself isn't always safe, but I'd rather go along with laws prepared by a group of people who are trying rather than be subject to one person's folly. If we go down it might as well be together, just like if we rise it is nice if we rise together.

It was a quiet and unassuming evening

Why do mystery and horror stories so often begin "It was a dark and stormy night?" We've all experienced a dark, stormy night, what is so mysterious about it? I know I tend to be home during those nights, only going out of the house if I have to. I don't want to be out in the rain. I imagine the same is true for most people. So why is this when all of the villains are out doing their work? Aren't they people, too? Don't you think they'd want to stay in on those nights?

For a storybook villain crime is a job, much like your job is your job. They don't want to go in to work if it means getting drenched on the way to the car. If they are like me and it is that dark and stormy, enough to mention at the start of a book, then they especially don't want to drive, I don't seem to see as well at night when it is raining. I think the villains would want to stay in on the dark and stormy nights. Perhaps if the start of the story when that business is going on is when the villains are planning their heist, or their caper, then I'll go along with it. There wouldn't be a better time to plan than on a dark and stormy night.

Some of you might be thinking that the stories don't always involve rational villains, so maybe that's why they are out on the dark and stormy nights. I'll give you that. It is not beyond reality to believe that there are irrational villains, and that these would be the ones cavorting on the dark and stormy nights. That could be a very real possibility. Perhaps these are the ones the stories are often involving. I still think there is an over representation of dark and stormy nights in horror and mystery stories.

If I was telling the story, I'd have it be a calm and unassuming evening, or perhaps even an afternoon, when the villain strikes. Especially after all of the priming that the other stories have done on us so that we automatically expect the worst when it is dark and stormy. My villain would certainly strike in the open, using the fact that people are inattentive in regular situations to their advantage. That's all I have regarding this topic at the moment. I was just thinking about it recently, how the dark and stormy line is so cliché in mystery and horror stories. I suppose I am done thinking about it now.

If it Ain't Broke, Enhance it

If it isn't broken, don't fix it…but that doesn't mean you can't enhance it. Where would we be in life if there weren't any genius mad scientists trying to improve upon the machines and tools we use every day? Doc Brown's DeLorean wasn't broken, but he sure fixed it! Regular strength Tylenol wasn't broken, but isn't maximum strength a little more efficient? Do we want to be content with how things are, or do we want something better. The same rule that applies to stuff and things applies to life. My life isn't broken, but can it be fixed (enhanced)? Of course it can. So can yours.

How do we define broken? Typically, something that is broken is unable to accomplish its purpose. A toaster that doesn't toast is no toaster. Likewise, a car that doesn't drive, a computer that doesn't compute, an oven mitt that doesn't protect a hand, these are all examples of broken things. An item created to perform a specific function which no longer performs that function is a broken item. Is that a satisfactory explanation? I say it is not. I've got something different.

A toaster that doesn't toast is no toaster. A toaster that toasts is a toaster. There are a lot of different types of things you could toast; it isn't a one size fits all realm. Bagels are different from bread and both are different from frozen waffles. Of course this is old news, and there are toasters with multiple settings for various types of toastable items. The point is that the toaster wasn't broken, in that it was still able to complete its intended purpose, but it was broken in that it wasn't able to toast the multitude of toastable objects with much efficiency. It wasn't completely broken, but it wasn't at maximum efficiency. This is where enhancements come in.

An enhancement makes something more capable of accomplishing its intended purpose. Toast settings on a toaster are an example of an enhancement. You have a selector switch to determine if you want more toast or less toast. Is a toaster without a selector switch broken? No. Does it accomplish its purpose? Yes. Does a selector switch make a toaster more capable at doing its job? Yes. Does a non-selector switch toaster hold its own against a selector switch toaster? No. Is the non-selector switch toaster broken now?

No, it really isn't broken. The point isn't to change the definition of broken, or haven't I made that clear yet? No. The point is that something doesn't have to be broken before we address how to make it more efficient. We can't wait around until the toaster breaks and then while rebuilding it we decide to enhance it. Well, we could, but why wait? That's the point. Why wait? There are many systems (such as government and formal education) which are limping along, not completely broken, but heavily damaged, and yet they still accomplish a portion of their purposes, so they are left alone. If we wait until they are completely broken we might not be in a state where we are capable of fixing them.

So maybe we do want to change the definition of broken, or maybe just use a different word. Nothing is perfect, and if it ain't perfect, then enhance it. That can be the phrase. "If it ain't broke, don't fix it" as a phrase is broken, so we'll fix it with an enhancement: "if it ain't perfect, enhance it!" Now those are some words we could all live by. We'll enhance our toasters, our DeLorean fancy-pants cars, our government, and our lives. None of these things are perfect, nor are they all necessarily broken, but they all can use enhancements.

I don't know how to enhance everything, if I did, I'd probably do it and I wouldn't be worrying about having a job and earning a Master's degree. I'd be making decorative cakes with my wife, just for fun, and all of the children we knew would have cool cakes and lots of cavities. Dentists would be our friends…parents not so much. Perhaps it is better that I don't have the answers and the financial fortune that seems to follow the best ideas in this country. If we even function as a meritocracy any more, I don't know if we even function as a republic democracy, fully. Back to the point, I don't know how to enhance everything, but I think if you want to enhance anything you need to get a full scope perspective of the thing. Sit it down, figuratively or literally depending on what it is, and then walk around it. See it from every angle. Get opposing perspectives. Learn all you can about its reason for being created, its capabilities, and its imagined accomplishments. When the right person gets the right item at the right time, enhancements will come.

Inspired by Ishmael...the Gorilla

The following are my thoughts and opinions. Some of them are based on things I've heard from reputable academic sources, others are just synthesized from my own thoughts. I started typing after reading the novel *Ishmael* (1992), by Daniel Quinn. In the book a man talks with a gorilla about what's wrong with the world. The gorilla is named Ishmael. He can't speak, but he is able to "talk" to the man's mind. It is an interesting book to read, and while I don't agree with the premise – what's wrong with the world is that humans exist – I do appreciate the different perspective and I do agree with some of the ideas that are brought up along the way.

There are many different philosophies and theories about life and why the world is what it is, perhaps as many different views as there are different people. I believe that no two people can be exactly alike. Fingerprints are never two of a kind, and I don't think perspectives can be either. They can be similar, perhaps fraternal, but never identical. I shouldn't say never, I don't like to deal in absolutes, they are beyond what I can safely defend or persuade in behalf of. I do think that individual circumstances (environment and experience, nature and nurture) make each person unique and individual when compared to every other person, or any other person. Taking it one step further, each person is uniquely individual when compared to their own self from any given moment to any other moment. There are many different perspectives, and I find many of them to be fascinating; I also find many to be frustrating. Most intriguing of all is that the most frustrating are often times the most fascinating.

I enjoy learning. New ideas, even the scary ones, are great. Challenge is the catalyst for progression, and I like to progress, or, to see progress in my life. Different ideas from those I hold to be the truth challenge me. I have to look at what I believe from another angle, to weigh a new perspective against my own in the scales of conviction. There have been many times when I have weighed my perspective against the perspective of another and found mine to be wanting. This is how I have learned. Interestingly, I first had to have this type of experience to learn how to learn. When after discussing differing opinions with me, a friend suggested that my tone in discussion, my choice of words, and my presentation of my perspective were of such finality that I did not present myself as open and willing to listen to anything else. I struggled for a while with this critique, but I was able to appreciate the criticism and affect a change in my delivery. As my delivery changed, so too did my perspective. I learned to learn, which is to say, I learned that in order to learn I must accept that there is something I can learn, and that I can learn those things from anyone, at anytime, and from any experience. I probably never would have thought of myself as un-teachable prior to that path of enlightenment, but in many ways I was.

In addition to learning that I could find education from diverse and sometimes unexpected sources, I learned that realization of personal convictions and perspective is of primary importance. I may have an affinity for a particular activity, but if I never realize it then it doesn't do me any good. I am a Christian. I accept the teachings of Jesus Christ and follow his admonition to try his words, to test and to prove his doctrine to verify its validity. I have learned as much about my beliefs from people with different views of faith and religion as I have from those of the same faith and religion as me. I have learned to be a Christian equally from Christians and non-Christians alike. This comes from being able to recognize that learning comes from everywhere, and from being humble and teachable. Though I thought I was open in discussions with my friend, she felt that I wouldn't allow for any possible explanation or philosophy outside of my own tightly held beliefs. Because of how I presented myself, I was not teachable. When I was able to overcome that wall I was holding up, I was able to be taught by her. She provided another perspective from which to view my own perspective, thereby allowing me an outside-in view of what I believed, or professed to believe in. This different perspective has helped me in cases since (and probably cases prior without me realizing it in this context) to study and reaffirm or dismiss personal philosophies, explanations, and beliefs.

One prime example of this pattern is simple, yet has had a long lasting and rather profound effect on me. I was once discussing snakes with one of my friends, one that I consider an informal mentor. I am not fond of snakes, never have been. I told him how I would kill snakes in my yard just at the sight of them. There seemed to be an instinctive aversion to the creatures. Though I knew the snakes were completely harmless to me, I killed them because they made me anxious. My friend thought this was deplorable and asked me how I, a self-proclaimed follower of Christ, could be a distributor of such wanton destruction of life. In that moment something clicked and I realized he was right. And in that moment I changed a little. I have never killed a snake since. This is a situation specific to me, it may or may not have any bearing on you, but for me it was a lasting lesson.

Education can come to us at any time, from anyone, and in any place. If we want to learn and gain wisdom it is for us to make ourselves teachable. Part of being teachable is preparing the mind for new information. Everyone has had the experience of not being able to recall some vital information at one time or another. Recall is the ability to retrieve information from memory. Remembering is something that I think we all do very well and without much conscious effort. Exceptions would be in cases of brain damage or in association with certain behaviors that might cause brain damage. But for most of us, the brain functions quite well and creates neural networks to encode information we obtain through our senses. Where we fail is in our ability to recall that information. This is why we need to prepare our minds. The neural pathways that store memories are like paths through the woods. The more you walk along a specific route, the more the way gets trampled down and becomes clear. The first few times you try to walk a path you might have a difficult time finding the exact same way. As you repeat the trip, and perhaps draw a map, it becomes more familiar to you and you can follow it with greater ease. If you then branch other trails off of it, or join existing trails to the new one, you find your ability to navigate the woods ever increasing. It takes repetition and familiarity.

Repetition and familiarity can prepare a mind or boost recall. In order to retrieve information you must do just that, retrieve information. Constant studying of topics you want to know well can serve as recall practice, as well as prepare the mind for new information. In the case of formal education it is easy to prepare, or prime, yourself to learn a topic. Read a book about cognitive psychology before taking the class. Outside of formal education it isn't any more difficult to do, just to know when to do it. We don't always know when specific educational experiences will present themselves, so it is hard to prime for them, but we can prime ourselves by constantly reading and learning about various things. I think that learning about anything will improve our ability to learn about something. But when you know a specific opportunity is on the way, start to research it. Here is where all of this gets tied together; more than one source of information helps you remember something so you can recall it with less effort at a later time. Just like having two perspectives in a conversation, looking at things from more than one source will aid in digestion of information.

Behind the Scenes

It has almost been a year since I started playing with a website called Helium.com. It is an article database compiled by user submitted content. I have written a few articles for it. I enjoy writing; I'll just say that now in case you didn't know. Recently I started writing an article to submit to Helium, but didn't seem to grasp the title I was writing to before I started writing. After I was finished, or thereabouts, I realized that I was kind of off the mark. You see, Helium suggests titles and then you choose one you know something about and write the article to suit the title. Since I felt like I missed the point I decided not to post it, instead I will post it here.

I give you my unfinished essay, of sorts:

The air around us is constantly full of waves. It is a constant barrage of energy. Cell phones, radios, and other communication devices emit various frequencies from point A which are then received by like devices at point B. Some receiving devices look for all signals of their own language, or, frequency, while other receivers look for signals sent distinctly to them. Signals are sometimes lost or disrupted or blocked entirely by environmental hazards or defects in transmitter or receiver. It is an invisible chaos of communication that abounds every day.

Thoughts in the mind are similar to the various types of waves zipping around us in the air. Some thoughts have higher priority than others and command more attention. Other thoughts are attached to physical sensations and may have the ability to disrupt even the highest of priority thoughts. With constant stimuli competing for the attention of our five senses, it can be a very challenging thing to maintain control of our many thoughts.

For some people, distracting thoughts can be quite a nuisance. Invasive and unpleasant thoughts, or irrational fears and worrying, plague many people. For others, the types of thoughts that distract their attention might not be troubling per se, but they do interrupt the focus of attention and can become frustrating. Depending on the frequency, severity, and type of distracting thoughts, a person may want to find ways to deal with them. In the case of frequent, distressing thoughts, perhaps the assistance of a trained therapeutic professional, or religious leader, would be appropriate.

Distracting thoughts for most people can be dealt with using simple techniques of redirection and processing. Imagine a waterway in your mind, there are many branches from the main body of water, with varying currents throughout. All along the banks of this waterway are thought topics. You are the pilot of a boat and you choose which areas of the bank to dock your boat and attend to the topic at hand. In dealing with errant thoughts, or distractions, you must remember that you are the pilot of the waterway in your mind. You have control over your thoughts.

One process of controlling your thoughts is to use redirection. Redirection is a good tool for when a thought comes to mind that you don't want to deal with at the moment. For example, if you were thinking about the financial report you need to complete for work, and then thoughts of the movie you saw last night distract you, try to redirect yourself by thinking of your financial report from a different angle. You redirect your focus. Remember, you are in control of what you focus on. If you need to focus on your work, but random other thoughts interfere, perhaps it is because you are bored and thinking about the focus topic from another angle might provide refreshment for your mind.

You can also redirect your thoughts by changing the distracting thought into a thought about your focus topic. Make destructive thoughts become constructive. When you are the pilot of the boat, you are at the helm, you control the direction. Sometimes a current will pull you in a direction you don't want to go, but with the right ability you can use that divergent current to your advantage.

Distracting thoughts can also be dealt with by processing them. Some thoughts aren't as easily pushed aside, especially ones tied to physiology. These thoughts might include cravings for addictive substances or behaviors. In these cases, sometimes it is best to recognize how you are feeling and process the thought. It is distracting to you because you do not want it, but by focusing on not thinking about it, you are thinking about it more. You have to attend to the thought, recognize it, control your reaction to it, accept that it is there, and put it aside. In the waterway analogy, sometimes the current might be too strong to steer out of, in which case you are going where the water is taking you, but once you get there you don't need to attend to the topic available. At the shore the current subsides and it is then that you can resume your previously intended course of travel.

Distracting thoughts range from mild to severe, from inane to distressing, and can happen at any time. Learning to control your thoughts and not let yourself become distracted will help increase your productivity and perhaps your peace of mind. Remember that every thought we attend to takes place because we generate it. If you have created the thought, you can erase it.

The Sleep Bone Connected to the...?

As of last Friday I no longer work the overnight job that was causing my sleep schedule such trouble. I have immediately tried to get back to a normal-person sleep schedule of being awake when the sun is out and being asleep when the sun is out. See that? We say the sun is out when it is "up" and shining it's light on us during the day, but wouldn't it make more sense to say it is out when we don't see it's light? That's what we do with light bulbs. If a light bulb is out then it isn't giving light, maybe, in the interest of congruence, we ought to say a light bulb is out if it is giving light. If we don't make this change then I will continue to say the sun is out when it is "up" and also when it is "down." It will lead to mass confusion! Regardless of how we call it, day is day and night is night; people sleep during the night and are awake during the day. I want to be people again.

It isn't as easy as that. I tried sleeping during the night, but I couldn't. I determined that my sleeping bone is broken. I figure I need to treat the situation like any broken bone, set it and forget it. But don't actually forget it; I only typed that because it rhymed. In order to set my broken sleep bone I think I need to determine what hours of the day I want to sleep and then put myself in a position to sleep during those hours. This means that even if I lie awake through most of the night I still need to be in bed. Setting a bone isn't exactly comfortable, nor does it automatically fix the break. It takes time.

The next step is to immobilize the break as best as possible. In terms of the sleep bone, I think this means that I don't change the hours I set for sleeping, which includes not taking naps. Just as a broken bone needs to relearn how to be a not-broken bone (I know, my wording is very technical, do your best to keep up) and how to handle the daily stress that would be put on it, whether that is walking or doing push-ups. Immobilizing the healing sleep bone will require a standard sleep schedule and no naps because naps will interfere with sleeping at night. Again, the healing process isn't instantaneous, and it isn't always comfortable.

I think a broken bone is a good analogy for an out of whack sleep schedule. I can't wait until I once again have my sleep schedule in whack. And now I must close this blog post and search Wikipedia to find out what it means to be in or out of whack. Good day to you.

Back to the Revolution

I haven't had Internet access for a few days, but now I do. The Internet man was supposed to come today between 8am and noon, so I figured I wouldn't see him and then I'd have to call and wait another week. But I was pleasantly surprised to see him at 9am, well within the boundaries of time they gave. Of course, he did come as soon as my wife and I were about to sit down to eat breakfast. I didn't mind the timing though as I was just happy to see him and be connected again so I could get today's assignment for school completed on time.

In other news, it has been a busy week and I have thought of a few things to write about, but I haven't written anything yet. I say this often. Usually a statement of this nature is followed by, "instead I'll just mention this." Today will be no different; I haven't written any of my recent ideas yet, so instead I'll just mention this. I walked into the bathroom earlier and there was a spider in the bathtub. It wasn't a menacing looking spider, so I didn't get scared. I watched him as he tried to climb up the wall of the tub.

The wall opposite the faucet is sloped up, a very steep slope, but less than 90 degrees. The spider was trying to climb up this wall, but kept sliding backwards. He would tentatively place his legs around in different places, trying to grab a good hold, and then attempt to walk. Either he would slide backwards, or fall over backwards. He wasn't having much success. Until at one point he made it up a few inches. I thought he might get it, but then he slid all the way down. It didn't occur to me then, but it does now, maybe he was just playing. Sliding was the purpose of his climbing. Maybe.

After that long slide he walked in the other direction. He stopped and just stood there for a bit. Then one of his forward legs moved to his head, or where I assumed his head would be, if he had one, I don't know spider anatomy. It was as though the spider was raising a hand to his chin which he then rubbed pensively as he attended to his predicament. It was a long moment before his leg returned to the tub floor. He then continued to sit. Perhaps thinking that spot as good as any to simply wait for food to come by.

I don't know the fate of the spider, I could probably go check and see if he is still there, but I don't want to. I'm sure I'll cross paths with him again. It is a small apartment we live in. More importantly was the direction my thoughts then went in. Spider-man scales walls, right? Like a spider? I guess there are a lot of different spiders and the radioactive ones have better climbing abilities than the standard house ones. Either that or if you put Spider-man in a bathtub he is powerless to climb out. He still has his super power web slinging ability, so I guess he'd be okay, but it wouldn't be from climbing.

I just realized the title to this post implies reference to *Back to the Future*. I'm sorry to report that it doesn't.

Functional Fixedness

What are you sitting on? Is it a chair? Maybe it is a bed, a sofa, a crate, an inflated rubber ball, a hammock, a stool, a large rock, an overturned bucket, a television, a horse, pile of clothes, or something else. Whatever it is, it is effectively a chair, because that is what you are using it for. I once had a roommate who expressed surprise when I was eating cereal in the evening. "That's a breakfast food!" he exclaimed. So what? You can only eat cereal in the first few hours after the sun comes up? Just as whatever you are sitting on becomes a sort of chair, you can eat whatever food you want at any time of the day, free of societal norms and associations. It interests me that some people would never think to eat breakfast in the evening, or would never think to use an overturned bucket as a chair. Some people are caught up in what is called functional fixedness, which is to be unable to see beyond the obvious function of an item.

A great example of breaking the confines of functional fixedness is the "son of the earth" (politically correct for hillbilly) who first used a saw blade for a violin. Chances are this was the result of some moonshine inspired goofing around, but either way, the saw was seen as being capable of more than its intended function of sawing wood. A common example in the literature for the subject is opening a door without a key. If you don't have a key, how do you open a locked door? You need to find another item that can perform the function, even if the item isn't intended to perform the function. Perhaps a credit card can be used to slide into the door jamb and pop the lock, or a butter knife for the same purpose? You could use the coffee table as a battering ram and smash the door down. The world is your playground, all items are interactive and your imagination is the limit.

I think functional fixedness is bad news. It is limiting and it shows a lack of creative thinking. I enjoy finding alternate uses for common items. Of course I can't think of any good examples, but I know that I often find alternate solutions when the preferred tool is unavailable. But as I can't remember any examples you'll just have to take my word for it. The point is to use your imagination and be creative when looking for solutions, whether because you need a hammer and don't have one, or because you can't figure out how to get along with a coworker. In any situation, a little imagination and creativity might be the right solution. As you start with finding new and creative ways to use ordinary objects you will develop the ability to come up with new and creative solutions to all of life's problems.

Hey! I remembered an example, although this is more of an example of lazy fixedness rather than overcoming functional fixedness. In fact, it hardly applies to functional fixedness at all. One time all of the spoons were in the sink and rather than wash one I used a punch bowl ladle to eat my Lucky Charms, sorry, I mean, me Lucky Charms. A ladle isn't typically used to eat cereal, but it worked. My motivation was laziness, but it was a good exercise of creativity, almost. It isn't that far of a stretch from ladling punch to eating cereal, but you get the idea, right? Of course you do. And this post is over.

The elders of the internet know who I am?!

I had forgotten how much busier I am when I have a job. It was a solid month between my last job and my new job, a solid, sweet month. Now I have a job again, and I really do enjoy it, but it takes up a lot of time. I am compensated for my time, and so the world keeps spinning, but it still is a lot of time. Blogging seems to have taken a back seat to living, which really is a contradiction of terms for the whole purpose of this blog. That's immaterial. I'm blogging now, while simultaneously drinking vanilla something or other flavored granola from a small, green plastic cup.

There is so much to write about, like my pondering on why we call wearing a costume for Halloween dressing up, while at the same time we call wearing a suit or formal wear dressing up as well. And when we wear sweat pants we call it dressing down. Think about the events you dress up for: job interview, church, funeral. Now think about the costumes you wear to dress up on Halloween: clown, psycho killer (one who kills psychos or one who is a psycho and kills others), skeleton. Now picture wearing each of those costumes in the order I mentioned them to the three events I mentioned, also in the order I mentioned them. It doesn't seem appropriate. Therefore, instead of saying "dressing up" to refer to wearing a Halloween costume, I suggest we start saying dressing sideways, or dressing crookedly, or dressing diagonally. Just a suggestion.

I could also write about the things I'm discussing in my grad program. I'm only a few weeks away from completing this first class which I started in the Education program and have since decided to switch to the

I/O psychology program. I need to finish this class and then I can switch. So for the time being we are discussing education and it is interesting. This week I read about Joseph Lancaster. He wrote an essay or treatise or pamphlet of some sort in 1803 regarding his thoughts on education reform. I liked what I read from the excerpts of it. I will, one of these days, read the entire thing and I think it will make me want to write a blog post about it. Along those same lines, I'm reading a book called "As a Man Thinketh" which I got free from Amazon.com for my Kindle. It is a fantastic read. I agree with everything James Allen has written. I think that is the author's name. Probably is. What? I'm drinking granola out of a cup! APA citations don't apply here! It's the Internet! Which brings me back to the title and a sense of Zen.

Today I nearly broke the Internet, at least for one small group out in the central time zone. I don't remember what state. You see, I work as a sort of tech support representative. Well, I got into trying to fix something that was well beyond my scope of knowledge and I broke the Internet. Or so we thought. Turns out I didn't really do something wrong, Windows did. So that was a relief, sort of. I still tried to do a corrective task that I really wasn't capable of doing. Such is the learning curve. I've only been there three weeks now.

It did lead to a fun conversation with a coworker about how IT and tech support don't really need to know what they are talking about, they just need to sound like they do. For example, if someone calls me and says "Here's the problem" and I say "Oh my no! That's terrible, I don't have any idea what you are talking about!" the person will become concerned and worried. They are calling me because they don't know how to fix a problem, and they expect that I do. If instead of declaring that I'm just as dumbfounded as them, I say "I see, let me try a few things," not only do I maintain their expectation, or hope, in my abilities, but I also give myself some room to work. I say "a few things" meaning that I have several options to try, in case the first thing I try doesn't work. This buys me some time to poke around and happen to get lucky at finding a fix before they start to wonder if I really know what I'm doing. It's a thin layer of silicon chips we walk sometimes in this industry.

The key is to sound confident and use words beyond the common understanding of the layman. If you start losing it, and you feel like the person on the other end is picking up on your incompetence, you simply open a configuration file and start scanning the lines of text which to the untrained eye seem like a bunch of junk. You can win a lot of points by pulling off the "config file scan" appropriately. It looks impressive and puts the perspective that you know more than the caller back into the mind of the caller. It's just a big game. Computers are interesting. They usually do exactly what you tell them to do, but sometimes they don't. And that's an exciting and entertaining thing.

If you are wondering about the title to this blog, locate the search bar of your favorite Internet browser, type in "The IT Crowd the Internet for Jen," the first YouTube result ought to be the one. Watch it. Laugh at it. Love it. The IT Crowd is a British comedy and it is highly humorous, although rather randy, just like most of their television programs. The clip I refer you to is clean.

Mixed Nuts

As I sat at the table after dinner my attention was drawn to the bowl of nuts left over from Christmas. The variety bowl of shelled nuts has served as a center piece/meal supplement for going on three weeks now. Next to it is a smaller bowl with the nutcracker and shell fragments. The process of shelling nuts has taught me a few things. First, I like the crazy looking nut that slightly resembles an alien spacecraft I saw on the *X-Files* or some such show once. I have no idea what type of nut it is, but I like it. The almonds are also good, but I think I prefer those smoked, or adorning chocolate covered coconut. The second thing I learned is that I will never again criticize or question the cost of shelled nuts you can buy in the store. Never again! Probably!

In the past, back before I tried my hand at cracking and shelling nuts, I often wondered why it cost so much money for a jar of nuts. But not anymore, no, not after realizing just how difficult it is to crack a shell and not smash the nut inside. Not after seeing how far the shards and splinters of shells explosively spread about after making the first crack on the nut. I learned to keep one hand wrapped around the shell and to apply pressure more evenly, but they still shatter in an out of control fashion. By experiencing the work that each little tiny nut requires in order to spring the tiny morsel from its woody cage, I will never again question the $25 price tag on an ounce of macadamias. In fact, I wouldn't even question if they started paying us to take the nuts in shells because it is so much work to shell them. It is probably cheaper just to give them away.

Well, this was a more humorous thought when I was telling my wife about it while cracking the nuts, spending minutes on extracting small fragments from the shattered remains. Your loss.

Oreo cookies and graduate statistics

75% of me really doesn't like stats homework, the other 25% hates it. I started out with the 13 pages worth of questions in good spirits. I was answering questions with ease as I was remembering the French-accented Dr. Deltoid (yes, a nickname), my undergrad research methods professor, and all that I learned in his class. I remembered distributions and measurement scales; independent and dependent variables, even what between-group and within-group mean. It was almost a joy, until I hit the part where I was given data and needed to organize it and create charts and tables. You see, in my undergrad classes (stats and research methods) we were required to purchase a program called SPSS. I purchased that program and complained quite frequently about how slow it was. Well, it turns out that the program is a million and a half times faster than I am at creating histograms and frequency polygons in Excel, manually. Can you believe Excel doesn't have built in functions to automatically create histograms from a grouped frequency chart? I know! [Actually, I found out months later that there are add-on tools for Excel that might be capable of doing those tasks]

Well, needless to say, but here I am saying it anyway, because this was the point of writing (negating the usefulness of ever saying 'needless to say' in any seriousness), I wish I had SPSS. I don't know if I still have the CD for the program or not. It could be in a box in my parents' attic, or possibly in a box about 10 feet from me right now, I don't remember, it could also be in a trash dump out in Idaho somewhere after I gleefully tossed it out when I left school. One of these days, perhaps tomorrow, I'll check the box here at the apartment to see if it is still in my possession, otherwise I'm seriously contemplating a 3 hour round trip to scour the attic for it. The alternative is to drop $60 for a new one year licensed copy. Come to think of it, that probably is the best option; I'll spend close to the same amount on gas driving to my parents' house. Even if I find that I do have the CD, I might not be able to run it because it is probably a limited use license and it has been a few years since I bought it. Well, such is life.

I'm glad to be finished with this assignment, and until I have SPSS, or until I look at what next week's assignment entails, I am going to be dreading week two of this class. At least I have some Oreo cookies to keep me energized.

Calendar

Muffin Man is a great Facebook status writer. I've decided to take some of his status updates and try to turn them into a comedy routine. Here is a bit based on his recent status...

Well, it's 2012, the year of a major political battle for the U.S. presidency, the year of the warmest January in recorded history, and the last year of existence as we know it, according to some. The Mayan calendar ends in December 2012. Since their civilization ended about a thousand years ago, I'd say their calendar did pretty well. I don't see how we should get so worked up about the end of a calendar made so long ago, I mean, I buy a calendar every year, sometimes with motivational pictures of kittens, other times dramatic scenes from the Harry Potter movies, and all of those calendars end in December. That's just what calendars do, they end in December. I don't open my new calendar each January, flip through it, and then exclaim, 'Happy New Year! See y'all at the apocalypse next December!' What it comes down to is we have more faith in an extinct ancient civilization to keep the time accurately than we do in Hallmark…

Vending Machine Education

Does anyone else feel at times that college is no more than a vending machine for a diploma? You put your quarters into that machine, one after one, and then maneuver the joy stick to direct the steel claw over to your chosen field of study and press the red button. The claw is released and (after a dozen or so more tries with a dozen or so more quarters) it grabs the diploma and drops it into the prize recovery area. It is perhaps a little more complicated than this, but I wouldn't say too much more. That's one way to see college as a vending machine, but not exactly how I initially constructed the idea.

I'm completing my weekly assignment for my current class, Statistics, for the Master's program I am enrolled in. I am at times a little less than attentive to the questions because I know they are not being graded. Each week I complete between 40 and 50 questions from the end of the chapters assigned for reading that week. The procedure is to answer the questions, submit them, and then receive a grade based on completion rather than accuracy. This is great...for when I don't want to learn anything. I answer the questions, some of them accurately, until I get low on time or interest, whichever comes first, although both usually arrive at pretty much the same time in some *Happy Days* comic fashion when Ralph "Mouth" and Potzie show up at the same door-step, at the same time, with the same discount store roses to take Mary Sue to the sock hop at the American Legion. The point is that I don't put a lot of effort into answering these questions. I accept full responsibility for this, but I can't help but notice there are some aspects of the program that make this sort of behavior possible for me.

The vending machine is marvelous. It is the hallmark of convenience. The best part about it is that it is unmanned. If I owned a vending machine I could spend an hour a week stocking it and retrieving money from it and call it a day. The machine does all the work. Here I compare the current process of completing assignments in this class. I answer several dozen questions and submit them. The instructor returns to me a grade. The instructor didn't instruct me, they simply gave me a reading assignment and indicated which textbook questions I should answer. In follow through, I receive a grade and a filled-in answer key. If I am motivated I can review my answers and find out how I'm doing. Of course since I am not very motivated, to say the least - only in regards to this topic, statistics, I'm motivated to learn otherwise -I don't review my answers to the questions after I get the answer key. I chalk it up to a combination of the condensed time frame for the course (8 weeks) and the difficulty of instructor/student interaction through an online environment, not to mention (yet I am?) I work full-time and have other responsibilities in addition to school. Still, it is slightly disappointing that I am required to put in this effort without substantial feedback and monitoring.

Don't get me wrong, I love to learn on my own schedule without someone breathing down my neck, and I often read and think about things for the purpose of educating myself, everyday in fact. The difference here is that I'm not paying anyone for my own educational pursuits. When I am paying someone and my progress determines my eligibility for a degree I expect more follow up and direction. This is like going to Plato (who I tend to disagree with his philosophies the more I read about them) to be instructed by this historically celebrated teacher, and then he hands you a paperback copy of *The One Minute Manager* (no offense to Ken Blanchard, I read the book and found it valuable, but in contrast with learning at the feet of a master, it doesn't quite compare). Perhaps a better example is going to Mr. Myagi and hearing him tell you he'll e-mail you some "neat vids" he found on YouTube to teach you karate.

I should get back to finishing my assignment now. The point is that I don't think online education should be like a vending machine, I'd rather it be like walking into the candy store in *Willy Wonka* with Gene Wilder. Rather than putting money into a coin slot and getting a foil wrapped chocolate bar, you drop a few shillings into the flesh and blood hand of an eccentric man who will then sing you a song and pour unwrapped candy into your hands with a small shovel. That's the kind of education I want!

Renewable Energy

I think it is interesting how much work and worry we put into energy, both fossil fuel and renewable. What would you say if I told you that there have already been countless civilizations who have mastered renewable, clean energy? It's true. Civilizations who would be declared archaic in comparison to our civilization today have mastered clean energy. The most ironic part of it all is that as we entered the industrial age we left behind the clean, renewable energy age. All of our advances in technology have made us more dependent on the diminishing (or so they say, but I don't believe it) resources such as oil.

Think about it for a minute, tractors today run on diesel fuel and do the job of oxen and horses from years past, which oxen and horses run on grass, water, and sunlight. There's your renewable bio fuels: grass, water, and sunlight. We are so far off the mark. Sure, medical advances, communication advances, all that, but do we really need it? What is life all about anyway? Couldn't we accomplish the core purposes without the Internet, the Kindle, Facebook, and Dancing with the Stars? We don't even know what the core purposes of life are any more, not as a collective understanding at least. And when you have sub groups that know the core purposes, they want to kill or convert anyone else who has a different concept of the core purposes.

We are spinning our wheels. I just spent three hours doing ridiculous calculations on numbers for my statistics final exam. Before that I spent 8 hours talking to people about computer software issues regarding electronic storage of image and loan application documents. All for a paycheck. All so I can utilize more diminishing sources of energy. I should say consume, rather than utilize. What did I accomplish today? Nothing, when you qualify things. I spent nearly the entire time I've been awake in front of a computer at work and then a computer at home. It was a beautiful Spring day, but I was inside for all of it except to drive the two miles to the office and back. I spent all of 30 minutes (and that's generous) interacting with my wife and that was to eat breakfast and dinner together. She was sitting a few feet away from me while I was doing my exam, but we weren't spending time together. How can a day be successful if all I've done is generate some ethereal numbers in my electronic balance for my bank account? All I did was consume non-renewable resources.

How about we start a new occupy movement, called occupy common sense? How about we occupy the ground and grow our own food? How about we occupy the Earth and use renewable energy to secure our basic needs and then spend the rest of the time interacting with each other in philosophical and educational pursuits? We don't need universities, textbooks, science labs, or the Internet to be educated. Oh well.

Look what I can do

I miss writing blog posts, but I've been pretty busy writing school assignments lately. I'd hate to go an entire month without posting anything, an entire month name-wise, I've probably gone more than 30 days at a stretch by now. So, in the interest of posting something for April, here is one of my recent school assignments, I chose this one because of my concluding paragraph. You can take the boy out of the regular whimsical revolutionary blogging, but you can't take the whimsical revolutionary blogging out of the boy...

The Fundamental Attribution Error and Social Psychological Theory

Making decisions based on judgment is at the heart of living. As we interact socially with people of various levels of familiarity, we are constantly making judgments of people whether we know it or not. We make our decisions based on appearance, observed behavior, or initial strains of conversation. The culture we are socialized into determines a lot about the judgments we make. Nationality, religion, political agenda, and fashion interests all play into the judgments we make about people. Social psychologists study these judgments and their accuracy in applying the term fundamental attribution error, which is that we are more likely to attribute a person's behavior to internal causes rather than external causes, interestingly the opposite of how we tend to attribute our own behavior. This paper delves into the cultural influence evident in the fundamental attribution error and applies the theory to recent social psychological research.

When happening upon a scene in public, we often don't know much about the setting and environment of that moment. When we see someone behaving a certain way in that setting we don't necessarily know why they are doing what they are doing, or how they perceive the setting they are in. What do we do in this situation? We are going to make a judgment about the person, consciously or not, and we will more than likely attribute the actions of the person to their personality, not their environment (Aronson, Wilson, & Akert, 2010, p. 99). When we see a young woman by the fountain downtown with her arms up like wings, twirling in circles, we will most likely think she is an outgoing and unconventional, if not worse, person. What we are missing is the camera focused on her filming her antics for a school video project. According to Changingminds.org (2012), "this can be due to our focus on the person more than their situation, about which we may know very little. We also know little about how they are interpreting the situation."

Various cultures reflect the fundamental attribution error in different ways. What makes this process so common is its focus on the person, rather than the situation, a common process among Western cultures. North America, primarily, represents Western cultural thinking, which is to focus on the individual and analytic thinking, while the countries of Eastern Asia focus on the bigger picture, including the environment in which something occurs (Aronson, Wilson, & Akert, 2010, p.104). Because of these differences, the fundamental attribution error is more frequently espoused in Western thinking societies. "Western culture exacerbates this error, as we emphasize individual freedom and autonomy and are socialized to prefer dispositional factors to situational ones" (Changing Minds, 2012). Other cultural factors, such as gender perceptions may play into the judgments we make. A man who is brought up in a misogynistic culture, upon seeing a woman in a traffic accident, will attribute the crash to the fact that she is a woman rather than seek for external influences in the accident, such as icy roads or vehicle malfunction.

An interesting study about attributing social behavior to personal qualities was conducted by Brumbaugh and Rosa in 2009. Looking at coupon use trends among different ethnoracial and socioeconomic groups, the researchers studied the results of embarrassment and cashier influence on the customer's use of coupons. This study doesn't involve the fundamental attribution error directly; instead it looks at the perception of the error in the minds of customers. In this case, the fundamental attribution error is made by a cashier, judging coupon use by different racial or economic groups as a reflection of the person, rather than their situation, in turn this judgment is perceived by the customer and leads to embarrassment and influences their use of coupons (Brumbaugh and Rosa, 2009). The researchers found that customer perceptions of judgment did affect coupon usage in statistically significant ways (2009). While the study's purpose was not to identify or apply the fundamental attribution error to consumerism, the theory is applicable. We can see in this study how the judgments we make about a person without fully comprehending a situation, thereby attributing behavior solely to internal factors, can influence how we will treat that person.

The fundamental attribution error exists and is influenced by cultural and socialization factors. Perhaps judgments of internal attribution based on observed behavior are unfair or inaccurate much of the time, but the alternative is to launch an investigation into any behavior we see and need to make a decision about. It might be unrealistic to expect such endeavors for everyday life. In some cases it might not only be unrealistic, but impractical or even dangerous to try to determine the environmental cause for behavior. If I come across a person wildly waving a sword around in the park, I'm going to assume the worst and steer clear of them. Even if their behavior can be attributed to a situational factor such as defending against a swarm of bees (as impractical as that would be), approaching for further investigation doesn't seem any safer than making a judgment based on internal attributions to the swordsman.

References

Aronson, E., Wilson, T.D., and Akert, R.M. (2010). Social Psychology (7th ed.). Englewood, Cliffs, NJ: Prentice. ISBN-13: 9780138144784.

Brumbaugh, A.M. & Rosa, J.A. (2009). Perceived discrimination, cashier metaperceptions, embarrassment, and confidence as influencers of coupon use: An ethnoracial- socioeconomic analysis. Journal of Retailing, 85(3), 347-362. Doi:10.1016/j.jretai.2009.04.008.

Changing Minds. (2012). Fundamental Attribution Error. Retrieved from http://changingminds.org/explanations/theories/fundamental_attribution_error.htm

I want peas...World peas

Homer Simpson once joined the Navy Reserve. In comical fashion he found himself having dinner with the Commander of the submarine he was serving on. The Commander asked Homer what he wanted more than anything else. Homer, with a bowl of peas just out of reach, responded "Peas." The Commander, hearing "peace" was thrilled, and asked how Homer expected to get it, to which he responded "with a knife!" He then used a knife to retrieve some peas from the bowl. The gag continues, but that should be sufficient for explaining the title of this post. Now on to explaining the body of the post.

What follows is my response to a discussion question in my online Social and Cultural Psychology class. This week is the final and then another class is finished along my Master's pathway. The question was regarding optimistic and pessimistic views of the possibility of global unity. Here is my response copied directly over from the discussion board wall:

I really wish I would have kept one of my books from a sociology class a few years ago. The book was by John Turner and in it he mapped out his theory of racial discrimination. He had a flow chart in the book that showed how discrimination leads to identifiability, which eventually leads to increased discrimination. I've always found this to be fascinating because to me it means that the more we focus on the differences and how they need to be accepted, we inadvertently increased the separation. You can't glue a broken vase back together by focusing on how broken the pieces are, you have to get some glue and put the pieces back together. Typically you'll need some sort of brace as well to hold it in place as the glue dries.

Now with global unity we can look at it in the model of a broken vase. It is an easy comparison to visualize with the jagged property lines between states and countries across the globe. We are all people, but we don't focus on that; we don't focus on the glued together vase, we simply keep to our own broken piece of porcelain and focus on how broken the rest of the vase is in comparison to our little intact piece. Many countries want to get the vase back together, but not for the sake of getting the vase back together, but rather in order to increase the size of their piece.

Lately I'm finding myself to be very pessimistic although I feel that I am a generally hopeful person. I don't believe I am a "downer" to other people. People seem to be generally entertained by me, so I don't consider myself a pessimist or depressing person. But my point of view regarding global unity would probably be classified as pessimistic. I believe that since we are all humans, we share a really strong bond of commonality. Global unity takes more than a familial tie, however. Global unity is going to require a great deal of compromise. As we have just discussed the differences and similarities between cultures based on Hofstede's values, we see that there are some dramatic differences in cultural motivations and practices.

A culture that believes in a central government that governs the masses is going to have a tough time melding with a culture that believes that the family governs itself and neighbors simply coexist in peace, because they do, without government intervention. Likewise, cultures where women are beneath men, and baby girls are sacrificed to appease the vain pride of the parents, will clash with cultures where human life is respected and all children, all genders are celebrated just because they are of our human family (although it seems like these types of countries are fewer and fewer these days). These types of differences in culture and other differences that are more extreme can't coexist in peace. One or the other has to give if the two are going to coexist. The question then becomes which aspect of each culture has to yield and which aspect gets to thrive?

Why is global unity difficult to imagine? Because there is too much selfish pride in the world. Until this is eradicated cultures will remain broken pieces of a vase. Focusing on the broken pieces of the vase will never get it back together. Some of the unique aspects of those broken pieces will need to be lost in order to reunite into one vase again. Assimilation is necessary to form one united culture. I don't expect to see this happen without a very influential uniting factor, such as war, disease, famine, or love. I think it would be great for the world to unite in love, but I don't think it will happen without some huge shifts in current trends. Until we have a global uniting factor, a common belief, I don't see it happening. We already share the same blood, which is a pretty intimate connection, but that hasn't been enough for the world to see past skin color and eye shape. As unpopular and divisive sounding as my opinion is, I don't believe unity will exist until the focus on differences is abandoned and the focus on similarities embraced. Please note I said "the focus on" and not the differences themselves. I am not supporting a culture of clones, but rather a culture of individuals with common goals and ideals. I think if people would forget themselves just a little bit, and reduce their need for competition, they would find that there are some basic beliefs we could all agree on without losing individuality and creativity.

How to fix everything

I found an interesting quote in a comment string under a news article regarding a current political event. The quote was posted as follows:

A democracy cannot exist as a permanent form of government. It can only exist until the voters discover that they can vote themselves money from the public treasury. From that moment on the majority always votes for the candidates promising the most money from the public treasury, with the result that a democracy always collapses over loose fiscal policy followed by a dictatorship.

The average age of the world's great civilizations has been two hundred years. These nations have progressed through the following sequence: from bondage to spiritual faith, from spiritual faith to great courage, from courage to liberty, from liberty to abundance, from abundance to selfishness, from selfishness to complacency from complacency to apathy, from apathy to dependency, from dependency back to bondage.

- Alexander Fraser Tytler (1747-1813)

A quick search in Google tells me that this is a composite quote, not necessarily by Tytler as the comment poster cites it, and possibly of unknown origin. I feel like I've been through this all before, finding a quote I really liked, searching for the author, and finding that it has been attributed to several people, throughout time, and across nations. Well, it isn't important who penned the words; the important thing is the apparent truth of them.

The cycle set forth, from bondage to faith to courage to liberty to abundance to selfishness to complacency to apathy to dependency and back to bondage, is prevalent in all aspects of life. You can find this cycle of behavior in your own life. It appears in individual behavior and in group behavior, and if you look into history, it appears in the course of large nations. What intrigues me is that it always seems to happen, and that it is clearly happening in the United States right now.

I can't fully imagine a war fought on U.S. soil, but some of the current events seem to point that way. Thinking about this cycle of bondage points that way, too, if we look at the U.S. over the last 60 years. There was great prosperity and abundance after World War II. There were ups and downs along the way, but for the most part, the latter half of the 20th century was prosperous. The result is Generation Y, intent on finding pleasure, immediate pleasure, in all aspects of life. They, along with many of the generation that made them, (I'm on the cusp between Generation X and Generation Y, so I don't know how I fit into this mess), therefore, we, are selfish, complacent, and apathetic.

We want services, but we don't want to pay for them. We know there are a lot of people struggling in the world, but we'd rather watch people eat live tarantulas in prime-time than figure out how to help feed the children being neglected down the street. We know that people are suffering, but we don't care. We are dependent upon the "gracious" hand of Uncle Sam. I have been thinking that the government has become its own entity that it was no longer made up of people, that it no longer represented the people. I hoped that the people still consisted of the types in the faith and courage part of the cycle outlined above. Now I wonder. Maybe the government really does represent the people. Maybe the greed and corruption we see in the government isn't some separate body from the people of this country, but is an accurate sample of the people of this country. If this is the case, it is time for a new declaration of independence.

Thomas Jefferson and the Continental Congress declared independence from the British Monarchy on behalf of the people living in the American colonies at the time. Great Britain fought against the rebellion, but lost. Human liberty won. Human liberty is now threatened again, but not by the control of a foreign government. It is threatened by the control of a domestic government; it is threatened by the people of the country. We are endangering ourselves. How do we declare independence from ourselves?

War? I can't picture what it would look like, and I hope it doesn't come down to that. But the alternative is found in changing the way we do business (meaning how we conduct ourselves in general, day to day), and this doesn't seem to be a realizable option. Without a change, without war, it will continue to stagnate and putrefy, and we will find ourselves in bondage.

As though we aren't currently in bondage, I believe we are. In our country of liberty, I am not free to own anything of my own accord. Most items are taxed at point of sale, and then again yearly through registration fees and property tax. I might buy a vehicle, but then I'm required to register it every year and be covered by insurance. If I don't buy insurance, I can be fined, another form of tax. Now we will enter a similar process with health insurance. Buy it or be taxed. I can "buy" property, but then I pay taxes on it every year. If I wanted to have my own farm on which I raised crop and animals enough to provide for my family, I couldn't do it unless I paid the taxes and licensing fees to do it. There is no ownership, there is only rental.

I might not be so unhappy about the arrangement if the rental fees I paid to the government were used for the purposes they are marketed to be used as, or at least, if the purposes they are used for were relevant to me. I understand property taxes insofar as they pay for local shared utilities and services. I can see the wisdom in this type of community living, what I cannot see the wisdom in is these monies being used to pay someone an extravagant salary and retirement. It has all gotten out of hand. And we've done it to ourselves. We have given up on life, liberty, and the pursuit of happiness in return for a little security on what we have at the moment.

At some point we gave up our faith, and relied upon our own courage. But that was imperfect and we got scared, so when we developed any kind of abundance, we safeguarded it, but not through faith and personal courage, through fear and reliance upon an outside influence. All we had to do was give up a little bit of our liberty in exchange. So we did. And then with the security it gave, we fell into complacency, and ever since the carpet has been being pulled out from under us, inch by inch, a little at a time, until now we are on the very edge, about to have it yanked out from under us completely. The sick joke is that we are the ones pulling the carpet! We are about to pull the carpet right out from under our own feet and then act surprised when we are lying face down on the floor.

We built a house of cards and it is about to fall over. Will we be able to rebuild that house of cards, or will someone else get to the deck first and change the game? In reality the game already changed a long time ago. While some were still working on the house of cards, others were slowly taking cards off of the house and reshuffling them in preparation for a new game. We can all buy in to the new game; of course, the ante is your freedom.

There is one answer, and it is found in that cycle describing our return to bondage. The path starts out in bondage, and the delivery from bondage is found in faith. Faith is the answer. The beauty of the process is that it can be restarted at anytime. We don't have to return to full bondage (remember, we are already in bondage), we can go right to increasing faith, and then when we are able to incorporate courage, and abundance, we go right back to faith. It can be done, but only if we eliminate selfishness. Again, the root of all problems is selfishness. Meaning the solution to all problems is humility. Further, the root and solution to all problems lies within each individual person in choosing how they will live and relate to other people. Now for the whimsical portion of this revolution, we have the power within us to affect this change; we have always had it, just like E.T., Dorothy, and Rocky IV.

Losing interest in Lost

It took some time, but I've finally bought into the craze that is ABC's TV program Lost. Well, "bought in" isn't accurate, "yielded to invitations to view for free online" is more like it. Originating in 2004 the series spanned 6 seasons and captivated audiences almost all the way through. I've been encouraged by friends to watch the series, but until about a month ago I never did. The premise of the show, based on having just finished watching the entire first season, is that a plane crashes on a seemingly uncharted Pacific island and the 40+ survivors deal with it. My wife and I watched the first season on Amazon Prime beginning in July and finishing up just a few days ago. That's my back story, now we'll return to my review of the show.

As I said, I have been encouraged by many people to watch Lost. Everyone was always careful to not give away any of the plot twists. Perhaps if they had I wouldn't have subjected myself to watching the entire first season. There it is, I've said it; I don't particularly care for Lost. It is interesting in its use of suspense, and I do enjoy the character development with the back stories, and some of the characters are just fun, but overall I find the series confused and disappointing. I don't say that it confuses me, just that the story line is confused on its own.

I do not fear revealing the surprises now as the series is complete and season one is 8 years old, plus I read a study that suggested plot revelations do not spoil a book or movie experience for those who have yet to read or view them. So I won't be concerned with keeping any secrets from you. The island the survivors are lost on is not your ordinary island. The plane was well off course and out of communication when it went down, so there is little expectancy that they will be found quickly, although many of the passengers hope for this. Overall the hope is sufficient that they delay searching for adequate food, water, and shelter for a few days. Amazingly, missing out on the basic necessities of life, and modern conveniences don't seem to have any effect on them. They continue to look and act very healthy (physically), for the most part.

But it is a TV show, so I don't get too caught up in the fantasy aspect of how well they are doing for being in such a fix. What does bother me is that every single person on this island, aside, perhaps, from Hugo "Hurley" Reyes, is a self-righteous, irrationally proud, prejudicial creep. Honestly, other than Hurley, I think the world is better off having this collection of nit-wits confined to the island and out of our hair. Yes, even though it is only 40 people, left to roam free throughout the earth, they would do some major damage. Hardly a full episode can pass without someone jumping to judgment and accusing someone of a heinous act, or someone says "don't tell me what I can't do!"

As I said before, I do enjoy the character development in the story; I just wish the characters weren't quite so ignorant. I think Lost could have been a great show, but what happened was the creators didn't think past the pilot episode. They though "let's do a modern twist on Gilligan's Island, but in a drama format instead of slap-stick, it'll be great!" So they got started writing, casting Jack the surgeon as the Professor; Kate the fugitive as Ginger; Sun the repressed wife of a mob-style hit man as Maryanne; Saiyd the former Iraqi Republican Guard communications officer also as the Professor; Shannon and Boone the crazy twins as the Howell's; Michael the divorced parent reuniting with his biological son as some form of the Skipper and also the Professor; and Charlie, formerly of rock band Drive-Shaft (and heroin addict), and the aforementioned Hurley, lottery winner and curse-bearer, as a split act Gilligan. Other characters too, some main, some not, but those are the Gilligan's Island comparisons for the most part. I got sidetracked on that.

Well, the creators put the show together, made a pilot episode with a good hook, and then realized they didn't have a real story to tell. Was it going to be Robinson Crusoe with a lot of people? Or would they let the Gilligan's Island comparison be obvious? They had no idea, so what happened? They made an invisible monster that rips trees out of the ground. They put a mysterious capsule buried out in the woods. There was a polar bear, just one, that charged a group of survivors early in the series. They even added a French woman who was shipwrecked on the island 16 years earlier, who was living, in seeming comfort, all alone for all of this time. And then there is The Others. Whispering voices in the woods that are later realized as unkempt sailors on a small boat in the final episode of the first season who kidnap a 10 year old boy from the bamboo raft. It turns out the island isn't so uncharted and deserted after all. Who knew?!

I don't really have a review for Lost. I liked some of the episodes, or at least parts of them, but overall I found my interest waning and my distaste waxing as each episode passed. The first season was a series of let downs at various stages in the haphazard story line. I was hopeful for different characters to take the lead and build a strong working community on the island. The resources seem to be there, they have knowledge from various walks of life, but the overall theme keeps turning out to be that these people are fatally flawed and incapable of working together. They each seem to have their moments of heroism, only to be shortly followed up with villainy or something. Granted, they are under profound stress and trauma, but it just seems like they are bouncing between extremes too quickly. Maybe the intent is to show that these are "real" people and subject to weakness and flaw, which I accept, but then they should be real people all of the time and not perform miracles one minute and not know how to tie their own shoes the next minute.

I think what it comes down to is that I'm jealous; one, because I want to live on a deserted island and see if I can survive, and two, I've never written a television show myself. So when I see plot twists instead of thinking "oooh! The suspense is thrilling!" I think, "no! you are doing it all wrong!" Because I envy their situation. Such as when Sawyer killed the polar bear, why didn't they try to eat it? Maybe because they still thought they would be rescued or because Locke hadn't busted out his knife supply yet. I don't know, but I wouldn't have let it go to waste. I don't know how bear meat tastes, but in that situation it seems best to find out. And other times they leave the story too full of holes. Who was Ethan? Where did he come from? Why was he helping Danielle? Why did he seem to have superpowers? Perhaps they'll explain it in the next 5 seasons.

Yes, I will continue watching the series, but under protest. I think they had a great story and it fell apart. They got scared and thought they needed invisible dinosaurs to keep people interested. Then again, maybe I'm the only one who sees it this way. If I am, I'm 100% okay with it. In my opinion Lost is not worth its hype.

Afterword

Ajax's Whimsical Revolution provided me with a great outlet for sharing creativity and exploring my ideas about all kinds of subjects. It even brought me a little attention along the way, and who doesn't like attention. I find that writing, or typing, or talking about what I think and feel helps me to better understand those things myself. For this reason I've continued my blogging, but I've tried to make it a little more organized. Please visit http://paulbrodie.wordpress.com where I continue to write regular posts about all things psychology, sociology and philosophy applied to living in today's world. Additionally, you'll find a cartoon gallery for your comedic interests and some links to my music for your listening pleasure. I've also begun to realize my childhood ambition of writing a book. This compilation of essays and thoughts was just the first self-publishing step. I hope to develop a collection of essays, short stories and eventually full length novels to my personal library. Personal meaning "written by me." But I guess you figured that out. Thanks for reading!

Made in the USA
Charleston, SC
06 June 2013